The Selected Poems of
George Daniel of Beswick

George Daniel
of Beswick

The
Selected Poems
of
George Daniel
of
Beswick
1616-1657

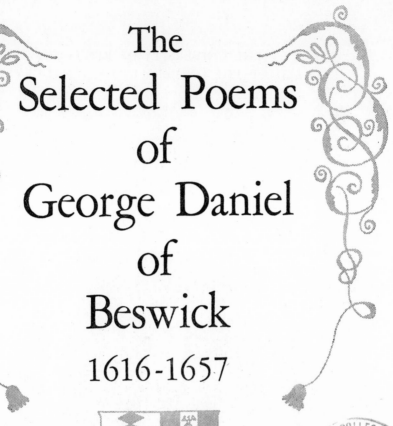

Edited by
Thomas B. Stroup

University of Kentucky Press

The publication of this book is made possible partly through a grant from the Margaret Voorhies Haggin Trust, established in memory of her husband, James Ben Ali Haggin.

The Library of Congress catalog entry for this book appears at the end of the text.

TO MY FATHER AND MOTHER

Acknowledgments

ONE NEVER CAN REMEMBER all who help, for much comes casually and incidentally—a conversation, a suggestion, or the long-suffering of a listener who patiently puts up with enthusiasms he does not share. For all such I am grateful.

The more direct helpers can the more easily be named. I am obligated to the officials of the British Museum for the privilege of using and photographing the manuscript and for permission to publish from it. I am even more obligated to the University of Kentucky Research Fund Committee for grants which enabled me to pay for the photographing and to have the work transcribed. I am indebted to the officials of the Margaret I. King Library of the University of Kentucky for many courtesies, not the least of which was the use of microfilm-reading equipment. I am grateful to the Reverend S. A. Cawthorn for generously showing me the records of his church at Kilnwick, Yorkshire. I owe much both by way of particular advice and general direction to Professor Fredson Bowers. I am indebted to Herman E. Spivey not only for encouragement and counsel but for more exacting help—that of reading the typescript itself. To no one do I owe more perhaps than Miss Louise Taylor, whose careful transcription and proofreading was equaled only by her patience with changes and reworking. My wife must be remembered for standing so often and waiting so well.

Lexington, Kentucky
February 26, 1958

Contents

Illustrations

George Daniel of Beswick

THE REVEREND ALEXANDER GROSART published in four volumes, for one hundred subscribers only, *The Poems of George Daniel, Esq., of Beswick, Yorkshire (1616-1657)* (Boston, Lincolnshire, 1878), the first and only edition of Daniel's writings. These volumes are physically worthy of the fine manuscript in the British Museum from which they were printed, but they leave much to be desired by way of text and notes as well as introduction. Few in number and widely scattered, copies of this edition are inaccessible to the general reader and not easily available to the scholar. Apparently only four of Daniel's poems have been printed elsewhere, three in *Rare Poems of the Seventeenth Century* (edited by L. Birkett Marshall, Cambridge University Press, 1936) and one in the first edition of *Understanding Poetry* (edited by Cleanth Brooks and Robert Penn Warren, New York, Henry Holt, 1938). The headnote to the three in Marshall's anthology suggests that a number of Daniel's poems "are worthy of rescue from the oblivion into which they have, for a second time, sunk." The present edition of selected poems of Daniel is a modest attempt at the rescue.

Aside from the edition and the reprintings mentioned, George Daniel has very largely escaped the eyes of critics and historians. A brief life in the *Dictionary of National Biography* and three notes upon allusions to Shakespeare in Daniel's poetry constitute the notice that he has received.[1] He would seem, therefore, to merit some little attention at this point—his life and works.

THE POET

According to the pedigree of the Daniel family of Beswick appended to Grosart's Introduction to *The Poems* and confirmed by the parish records of Kilnwick, George Daniel was born on March 29, 1616, at Beswick, a manor, township, and chapelry in the parish of Kilnwick in the East Riding of Yorkshire, on the highroad from Great Driffield to Beverley, two miles northeast from Lockington and some six miles or more north of Beverley.[2] His father was Sir Ingleby Daniel, once matriculated at Caius College, Cambridge, an active supporter of Charles I against the forces of Parliament; his mother was Frances Metham of Pollington, Sir Ingleby's second wife. His older brother William died before Sir Ingleby; hence George succeeded to the manor of Beswick upon his father's death, probably in 1644. His younger brother Thomas, apparently much admired by George, became first a coronet in the army of King Charles and then, after the Restoration, Sir Thomas Daniel and High Sheriff of Yorkshire. George married Elizabeth, daughter of the well-to-do William Ireland of Nostell, Yorkshire, by whom he had an only son, George, and three daughters, Frances, Elizabeth, and Girarda. The poet died on September 25, 1657, and was buried in the churchyard of All Saints, Kilnwick. George, the son, attended Magdalen College, Oxford, but died without issue and was buried at St. Giles-in-the-Fields, London, on March 16, 1664/5. None of the children of the poet's daughters lived. Sir Thomas, thus, succeeded to the manor. He left one son, Ingleby Daniel, "last Heir Male of

[1] Homer Nearing, Jr., calls attention to Daniel's reference to Shakespeare's *Richard II* in *Trinarchodia* (*Notes and Queries*, CXCI, 46-47); Lucy Toulmin Smith (perhaps at Grosart's instance) cites this same reference and the one in *A Vindication of Poesie* in *Shakespeare's Centurie of Prayse* (New Shakespeare Society, Series IV, no. 2, 1879); and the editor of *Choyce Drollery, Songs and Sonnets of 1656*, being Vol. III of *The Drolleries of the Restoration* (London, 1876, pp. 280-81), merely quotes the passage from *A Vindication of Poesie* in which reference is made to Spenser, Sidney, Donne, Jonson, and Shakespeare.

[2] For the facts concerning the family and the life of George Daniel, I depend upon Grosart's Introduction; the parish records of All Saints, Kilnwick; *Le Neve's Pedigrees of the Knights Made by King Charles II, King James II, King William III and Queen Mary, King William Alone and Queen Anne* (edited by George W. Marshall, *Publications of the Harleian Society*, Vol. VIII, 1873, p. 157); *Kelly's Directory of the North and East Ridings* (p. 542); *Yorkshire Pedigrees* [Vol. 1] (*Harleian Society Publications*, Vol. XCIV, 1942, p. 135); *Alumni Cantabrigienses* (compiled by John and J. A. Venn, Part I, Vol. II, 1922, pp. 7ff.); *The Victoria History of the County of York* (edited by William Page, London, 1907-1925, Vol. III, p. 419); *The Dictionary of National Biography* (the article on Daniel was written by the Reverend J. W. Ebsworth); and the records of the Church of St. Giles-in-the-Fields, London.

that ancient family," who died on February 26, 1710, and was buried in the chancel of All Saints, Kilnwick. So much is known of the poet and his family.

Other biographical matters, events in his life, his habits, and the qualities of his taste, can be learned in some measure from his verse. From it we conclude that Daniel was no soldier, but a retiring gentleman of cultivated and scholarly tastes, a would-be seventeenth-century Horace, loving chiefly his reading and painting, his fields and his pastures. It seems that at one time his wife's fortune saved the fields and pastures from his creditors. As a young man he seems to have borne the usual love affairs in the usual manner of young poets: he addressed conventional lines to his Sylvia, Cynthia, and Pudora; now and then he expressed a fleshly feeling for one or the other; and at one time in a very ecstasy of vexation he rejected all for Nicotiana, his faithful tobacco pipe. He invites a friend to visit him, promising good food and drink, and he humorously chides another for falling asleep while George read his verses aloud to him. He plays with platonic love in some nine poems, but finds that it satisfies no passion and rejects it. We learn from title pages furnished in the manuscript that his poems were individually circulated among his friends. Though Daniel seems to have had a substantial formal education, we do not know where he got it. References in his poems indicate the usual readings of classical poets required of the public-school boy; but his acquaintance with contemporary English writers suggests something more—an unusual interest in the poetry of his own day, which may have been stirred by personal association with the poets. And yet there is little direct evidence (he probably knew Sir Thomas Browne in person) that he knew the men of letters of his own time except through their writings, and it seems unlikely that he traveled far or frequently. Visits to London and to the universities and an occasional trip to Beverley, Hull, and York constituted perhaps his chief journeyings. In his poems he repeatedly expresses content in his quiet rural seat and distaste for the unquiet splendor of court and city.

And though he supported Charles' cause and honored

Thomas, his soldier brother, he himself remained at home "to sing away, the Time's uncertaintie." He was much grieved at the fall of the monarchy and the rise of Parliament and Cromwell, believing the ancient liberties now either lost or in great jeopardy. He was fearful of the Commonwealth, and he wrote in such a long poem as *Trinarchodia* (a didactic chronicle in three parts dealing with the reigns of Richard II, Henry IV, and Henry V) of the disastrous political events of his own day in terms of other times. His *Polylogia,* a series of pastorals (represented by "The Fourth Ecloge" in this volume), forms a thinly veiled satire or allegory dealing with the usurpation of royal powers by Parliament. Yet he was no blind worshiper of monarchy. He says that "Tyrants must be unking'd," and calls upon God to "destroy the Seat / Of Majestie; if Majestie forget / Thy Power, or scorn thy rule." He says also, "I hate a servitude / Either to Might, or to the Multitude." True liberty, however, is not in the gift of government.

Apparently his reading was wide. Among the ancients he knew Horace, Ovid, Virgil, Tibullus, Marcus Aurelius, Lucian, and others; but chiefly he was a devotee of Horace and Virgil, the pastoralist. Among the moderns he mentions Sannazaro, Petrarch, Tasso, Dante, Ariosto, du Bartas, and du Bellay. He says proudly that he is a "son of Ben," and praises and imitates Jonson frequently;[3] he refers to Chaucer (though not favorably), Sidney, Spenser, Beaumont and Fletcher, Shakespeare, Donne (directly once and indirectly and by imitation many times), Drayton, Samuel Daniel, Wither, Suckling, Carew, Randolph, George Herbert (in a poem in Herbert's honor), Ogilby, Sandys, Habington, Stapleton, May, Digby, Shirley, Sir Thomas Browne, and several others. He reveals himself as on the side of the moderns in the incipient controversy over the relative merits of ancients and moderns. Chaucer has little claim to be the father of English poetry; Spenser was great enough to have furnished Alexander his Homer, and should not have been allowed to die a pauper; Sidney was a sweet

[3] It is just possible that Jonson visited Beswick as he went through Yorkshire on his famous walking trip to Scotland in 1618-1619.

singer; Donne was the King's great prophet, as referred to in the poem in honor of Herbert; Beaumont and Fletcher, great dramatists, were of equal merit; Shakespeare was good at comedy, though he should not have besmirched Fastolfe by making him a buffoon; Herbert's *Temple* is incomparable; the turncoat Wither's fruit has withered; and Browne's *Religio Medici* reveals a freeborn mind. He shows his acceptance of the Copernican system in *Trinarchodia* and elsewhere. Such is a sample of Daniel's readings and his opinions of them. His poems are full of echoes from the poets, especially from Donne and Jonson.

Three other subjects of his verse reveal the man. Daniel had a genuine regard for the landscape about him and the activities which went on there. Even today the countryside retains some of the pastoral characteristics noted in his verses. He records such details as the lamb leaving its mother's teat to play, not quite the sort of detail one copies from a classical pastoral model. Since he was much interested in hawking, Daniel's poetry abounds in allusions to that popular sport and images drawn from it. As one might expect from a look at the pictures in the manuscript, painting furnishes another subject for Daniel's verse. No less than seventeen poems deal in one way or another with the technicalities of this art. A series of six with such titles as "The Designe," "The Colouring," and "The Shadow," though they draw their terminology from painting, are actually attacks upon dictatorship, the analysis of a portrait being used to reveal character. Daniel also makes frequent reference to artists, especially Michelangelo, Titian, and Van Dyke.

A third subject is less easily defined. One might perhaps loosely term it philosophy, or that which "brings the philosophic mind." Daniel is concerned with the large speculative issues of the day. He was perturbed by the problem of flux or change (doubtless he had read Spenser's *Mutabilitie Cantos*), with the decay of the world or with the break in Nature's chain of being, with the coming of the new science and all that the age of doubt implied. He follows the metaphysical fashion, too, in the choice of imagery. For instance, he has a poem, not unlike Donne's, in which the basic image is the compass—only his is the loadstone compass. In another he refers to logarithms to elaborate a complicated arithmetic image. In "The Userper" he gives a succinct picture of the Chain of Being: " (For I was raised above the common Light / ... where we eas'lye see / All formes at once, . . ." What he thought to be the coming of anarchy in the fall of the monarchy and the rise of the Commonwealth was illustration enough of the decay of the world, and the opening *Addresse,* a bitter poem, indicates it. The vanity and folly of human wishes, often referred to, are expressed at some length in *Vanitie.* Man's hope lies not in political freedom, but in cultivating inner happiness. As he says in "Idyl I" of the *Idyllia,* liberty is an *ignis fatuus,* not to be found in governments: "to make it sure / Is from our selves; the inward mind Secure, / Affects not giddy noyse, . . ." His imitations of Jonson and Donne led to satire and to doubt. His poems treat most of the subjects for poetry current at the time. Possibly he had no very original convictions; certainly he was highly imitative. Yet he was aware of what was happening and shows a lively interest in most that occupied thoughtful men's minds in his day.

A country gentleman of the East Riding of Yorkshire, Daniel was interested in friends and farming, in hunting and hawking, in painting and books, in the new ideas of his time, and in the evil days now fallen upon the monarchy; he sang his time's uncertainty and consoled himself with sweet content drawn from his country seat and inner liberty drawn from philosophic reflection, the common solution of his day—perhaps not a bad one at that.

THE POEMS

Repeatedly Daniel tells us that his best poems, and apparently the greater number of them, were burned and thus lost to future generations. However that may be, those remaining constitute a body of verse quite sufficient to indicate the range and scope of his efforts, if not his ability. This fact would be at once apparent if the present edition could include them all, or at least one of the longer poems. Since to include them is impracticable, however, it will be of interest to give briefly some idea of the scope and variety of his work.

By all odds the longest of Daniel's poems is *Trinarchodia*. Furnished with separate title page in the manuscript and dated 1649, it is a didactic and allegorical verse chronicle in three parts dealing with the reigns of Richard II, Henry IV, and Henry V, and resembling the chronicles of Samuel Daniel. It is made up of 1,140 six-line stanzas, rhyming *ababcc*. Much of it is labored; some of it is obscure; but an occasional passage is effective, and here and there patches of gold break through, as in the comment on the dying Henry IV:

> Now the Blacke Cloud gathers upon his Orbe;
> And the Refractions of his Spirit Gild
> Only the Hemme of Life.

Such passages occur frequently enough in this and others of the long poems to make regrettable their omission from this collection.

Vervicensis, dated 1639, is an uninspired complaint of the ghost of the great Earl of Warwick as he stands "in the horrid Vale / Of Erebus," imitative again of such poems as Samuel Daniel's *Complaint of Rosamond* and the tragedies in the *Mirror for Magistrates.* Slightly veiled parallels between the political situation in Warwick's time and Daniel's give point to the piece. It is made up of 92 stanzas of ottava rima.

The Genius of this Great and glorious Isle (1637) was recovered from an imperfect transcript preserved by a friend, we are told, the original being lost. It is comprised of 104 stanzas of rhyme royal. In defense of Charles against the rise of the Commonwealth, the Genius of Britain appears to the poet and reviews for him the history of the intestine wars of the country, celebrates the great reigns of Elizabeth and James I, and concludes with a paean in praise of Charles I. Few passages in the poem will today stir the reader to patriotic fervor.

Daniel's paraphrase of *Ecclesiasticus: or, The Wisedome of*

Jesus, the son of Syrach (1639) takes up some 160 pages in rhyming couplets, with an induction of more than a hundred lines. The quality of the verse seldom rises above its original, but the wisdom of the work obviously held a fascination for the poet, as for other men of his time, especially those passages having to do with the wise ruler. So much for the longer poems, all of which I have omitted.

Taken as a whole, the best of the shorter poems are found in the *Scattered Fancies,* a collection of fifty-nine odes with a sort of envoy appended. These range widely in subject matter and in form, but usually deal with philosophical or reflective matters, and the form varies from four-line stanzas with lines of assorted length and rhyme patterns to twelve-line stanzas of just as assorted lines and rhymes. These are of such diversity and intrinsic merit that all of them are included in this edition.

Of the *Polylogia; or, Several Ecloges* (1638-1648), only one can be included, that "Spoken by Damon, and Amintas!" There are five of these rather long pastorals written in the conventional form of dialogs between shepherds, each ending with a song, and dealing with such subjects as country versus city life, sweet content, the lessons to be learned from nature, platonic reflections upon the revelation of true knowledge, "Love," the sin of drunkenness, an allegory upon the evils of Parliament and the Commonwealth, and the heroic decline and fall of Charles I. In these are some of the best of his couplets, many of which are bitterly satirical.

The next important group of poems is *Idyllia: The Distemper* (undated, though certainly late in Daniel's career), a series of five "Idyls" in iambic pentameter couplets. Connected in thought, they are satirical and philosophical reflections upon government, man, and the nature of freedom, the general conclusion being that only the "inward mind Secure" is truly free. Among these one finds some of Daniel's most perceptive passages and some of his most arresting metaphysical imagery. Among them also are some of his most obscure lines. "Idyl 4" only is included in this edition. Following these in the manuscript is a most unusual series of six poems having to do, ostensibly, with painting, but actually with revealing the picture of the King in his seditious land.

Love Platonicke (1642) is called "A Small Poeme." It is in reality a series of eight short odes (all included in this edition), with varying and extraordinary stanzaic structure. The first, "To Cinthia; coying it," for example, is made up of five stanzas of ten lines each, rhyming *aabccbddee,* with the lines varying in length from two to five feet. Contrary to what Grosart says of this group, they do not "throb and burn" with real affection, wrath, or despair; they are rather light, if not playful and humorous in tone. So is the delightful *Woman Charactred,* representative of yet another genre.

Such poems as *An Addresse* and *To Time and Honour,* in iambic pentameter couplets, might be called essays in verse, the one on the times, the other on literature; and so might *A Vindication of Poesie,* in six-line stanzas rhyming *ababcc,* an account of Daniel's reflections upon the poets of his own and earlier times. These remind one again of Samuel Daniel, of Sir John Davies and Fulke Greville. Most of the other poems may be considered occasional. Among them one finds two upon the writings of Sir Thomas Browne, whom the poet professes to know; one upon Wither, a biting "Ænigma"; two in praise of Ben Jonson; one upon Herbert; "An Essay" citing the work of recent English poets; an excellent Horatian "Pastoral Ode" celebrating rural life; and several upon country sports, weather conditions, and philosophical matters, such as the Donne-like "Magazine" and "The Userper."

This brief review gives some indication of the range of Daniel's subject matter and the variety of his verse forms. It suggests also the number of poems necessarily omitted. Generally speaking, the omissions are the longer works; they are likewise the poorer works. And though they have their bright passages, they fail to sustain for long any great degree of poetic excellence. It is thus fortunate that our restrictions upon space do not cause similar restrictions upon excellence. Most of the shorter poems, the better poems, appear in this volume. Here one may also find poems representative of most of Daniel's ideas and interests, from his hawking to his platonism, from his enthusiasm for painting to his despair at cosmic decay. Our collection, then, attempts to give the reader at once the best of Daniel and the poems best calculated to place him in his period and to reflect his thought.

Something must be said about reading Daniel. Some of his poems remind us of the verses of Lord Herbert of Cherbury and are of about the same quality as his. Like his, they often resemble the poems of Donne, no less his master than Jonson. But being without Donne's genius and skill, he sometimes does ill what Donne did well, namely, write elliptically and yet, for the careful reader, clearly. One must take seriously Daniel's own warning in his *Carmen Protrepticon; Lectori* prefixed to *Scattered Fancies,* in which he asks that the reader "Weigh everie word and everie Sillable" and repeat his reading, looking always for "Another Sense" behind the literal. As a matter of simple fact, the obscurities may often be cleared up merely by the insertion of relatives at proper places in the reading. Since the obscurities are seldom of greater difficulty than this, it seems unnecessary to add notes of explanation or clarification in the editing.

Finally, no one will claim for George Daniel a front seat among the poets of England; yet most would be willing if not anxious to allow him a back one, for as yet he has none. Although his verses are not great, yet they merit as much as those of some of his contemporaries which have been given attention. I refer to such poets as Herbert of Cherbury, or Alexander Brome, or Habington, or James Graham, Marquis of Montrose, or Flatman and half a dozen others who have places in Saintsbury's *Minor Poets of the Seventeenth Century.*

Daniel's main difficulty was in sustaining his muse. He seems to have grown impatient, as he tells us in several poems. He often composed line for line, getting a clever or startling idea to start with and a good line, but losing the idea later and neglecting to polish the lines. For example, he begins "The Userper" with "I saw the World; and wondred at the Sight; / (For I was raised above the common Light . . ." but unfortunately he could not sustain this level throughout. And even in "Ode XXIII" of *Scattered Fancies,* an exquisite lyric on the robin, the last two lines fail to make a good end. Daniel, nevertheless, often shows a fine sense of structure, as in such poems as *Proportion* and *Love Platonicke,* where balance is nicely sustained. And now and then he breaks through with such lines as these on the final dissolution of the earth in "Ode XIII" of *Scattered Fancies*:

> The mightie Elephant, and Mouse may run
> An Equall race;
> And in this case,
> The Heliotrope, may live with the last Sun.

THE TEXT

The text of this edition is based upon British Museum Additional Manuscript 19,255, a fine folio volume bound in blue morocco with gilt edges. In the *Catalogue* it bears the title *The Poems of George Daniel.*[4] In it appear five oil paintings done, it would seem, by the author himself. He implies as much in the poems and in them shows himself also to be uncommonly interested in the subject of painting. These pictures are a frontispiece of the poet shaking hands with his brother Thomas, a bust of the poet with the Daniel coat of arms above on f6[r], a half length of him seated in his study wearing a massive beard on f152[r], one of him in a Roman toga seated with inkpot and manuscripts about him and a rural landscape for background on f112[r], and one of a nude nymph, a sort of vision of one of his fancied mistresses, perhaps his Pudora, on f165[r]. Here and there throughout the manuscript are pen-and-ink

---

[4] The British Museum acquired it from the collection of Edward Lord Viscount Kingsborough, sold in Dublin in 1842. Kingsborough seems to have bought it from a man named Thorpe, apparently a Cambridge bookseller, who got it for £22 10s. at auction on December 9, 1833, from Sotheby's. Sotheby had it from the Caldecott Collection, but how it came into the hands of Thomas Caldecott we do not know. (See *Catalogue of Additional Manuscripts,* British Museum, Mss. 19,255.)

drawings of shields and coats of arms of the Daniel family. Separate title pages are made for the longer poems and for the collections, such as *Scattered Fancies*. Grosart says that the manuscript is in a single hand, and Sotheby's catalog lists it as "autograph." But neither is correct: clearly the work is in two hands, the second scribe's work beginning on f135 with the letter to the poet's brother "T.D." This letter and the remaining poems could possibly be in the hand of the poet, as well as the signatures affixed to some of the poems and perhaps a few insertions in the margins. But there is nothing except the letter itself to suggest this possibility. It seems likely also that the commendatory poem, "To his honoured friend the authour Upon his poems," by Thomas Crompton is in Crompton's own hand. In many cases the poems are dated; in some few, the originals being lost, we are told that the author had to rely upon copy furnished him by friends. Apparently the manuscript, in most places easy to read, was prepared for publication.

But if it is legible, its meaning is not always clear. The conventional abbreviations aside (and they furnish no problem), the punctuation, as Grosart found, is troublesome. Especially is this true of the first copyist's work. But neither scribe is either conventional or consistent. Both overpunctuate, sprinkling commas about almost indiscriminately; they seldom use the period, but make the semicolon and the colon serve both primary pauses and stops; and though they are conscious of run-on lines (as the poet intended), not infrequently they drop a comma or a semicolon at the end of a line where no break could possibly occur. Hence, in spite of one's efforts at a conservative text, one finds it necessary to exercise considerable discretion in handling the punctuation.

I offer a text, therefore, somewhat modified from the manuscript. I have tried to reproduce faithfully the spelling of the original and to follow the capitalization consistently, raising from lower case to capitals the first letters only of those proper nouns and adjectives the copyists failed to raise in keeping with their general practice, and to make the first letter of a line invariably a capital; to transcribe as *F* the *ff* of the manuscript and reduce long *s;* to write the vocalic *v* as *u* and the consonantal *i* as *j*; to lower all raised letters and write out the abbreviations of such forms as y^e, w^{ch}, w^{th}, etc.; to double the nasals *m* and *n* where the copyists use the contraction, as $\overline{com}on$, for example, such idiosyncracies being merely scribal. These modifications are made without note. It has been more difficult, but quite as necessary, to alter somewhat the punctuation. Periods have been placed at the end of stanzas, where semicolons and colons appear in the manuscript (unless, of course, the sense runs on), at the end of predications where colon or semicolon would confuse, and at the end of poems. Punctuation has been eliminated at the end of lines where the sense continues without break or pause, so as to maintain consistency. Indiscriminate use of the comma has been eliminated, though caesural use of this mark has been allowed where not utterly confusing; uses of the question mark and parentheses and punctuation marks with parentheses have been regularized; apostrophes are neither added nor deleted. Throughout, the practice has been to make the punctuation as consistent as possible with the copyists' own practices, holding them, within the limits of readability, to their own standards. These modifications are made without note. Hence the textual notes are very few, and record only those changes in punctuation which might conceivably change the meaning intended. Needless to add, they do record all verbal emendations and questionable readings. The attempt has been to present a slightly modified old-spelling text.

A word remains to be said of Grosart's work. It has been of little use in the preparation of this text. His occasional misreadings have made him unreliable; and perhaps only once has his work been useful in deciphering or clarifying. His changes in the punctuation of the original are not always an improvement. His text has, nevertheless, been compared with the manuscript; and if ever his emendation is chosen deliberately, it has been duly recorded. In the explanatory notes, on the other hand, his work has at times been helpful and timesaving. Here again, wherever his notes have been used, that use has been recorded.

A<small>N</small> ADDRESSE:
BY THE AUTHOR:
NOT IMPERTINENT TO THE FOLLOWING POEMS;
AU LECTEUR

P<small>HANCIES</small> <small>ARE</small> but our owne; and though wee give
Em birth; perhaps they have noe right to Live.
Why doe wee wast our Inke, and oyle, in vaine?
Wasting our Nights, and Dayes in fruitles gaine
To bring a Monster forth? a Prodigie?
Or Strange Chimæra, of our Fantasie?
What End have wee in this? ist not Enough
If to our Selves, wee our owne Follies know?
If wee poure out, for other Men to Eat
They'r full, as well as wee, with their owne Meat?   10
The World's a tottring Stage; and Mankind All
Is but one Antike Individuall;
From time to Time, the Same; noe Age can boast
The better Interlude; for what wee most
Admire, (before our Selves) or what we lest
Can Judge of, (after) has nor worst, nor best.
This Mockshow, this Coloss, this Maisterpeice
Of Nature, (as wee call it, when wee please
Our partial frailties) is that bruitish Thing
Degenerate, Foolish, giddy, wavering,   20
Voluptuous, Bloodie, Proud, Insatiate
Lump of Corruption which they wondred at
Twelve Centuries agoe; and Time shall bring
To its last point, just such another Thing.
There is noe wonder; if within the Sphere
Of Nature, ought Irregular appeare.
Wee are that odde Incorrigible peice
Of Error; tis within us, the Excess,
Defect, or what wee call Deformitie
To hinder Natures first made Harmonie.   30

. *I* .

This, when I looke at; and my Atome take
(A Sand of the rude Heape) I seeke to make
It cleane; and softly rubbe away the Slime;
I sleeke it Faire; and weare it, for a Time
My Boast, my Jewell; or more Ideot-like
I sett it in my Cap, where all Eyes Strike
Upon it; and I foole; am pleas'd to heare
Them rate it high; as though this Graine did beare
Proportion to a Piramid; this clawes
My Nature, for a while; but Time, (which drawes   40
All Things to Irksomenes) brings in a packe
Of Vanities, whil'st I forgett this Knacke.
Careles, I lay it by; whil'st the rude Heape,
(Which rolleth ever) it away doth Sweepe,
Into the wombe of that insatiate Gulph
Which Lethe, some doe call—

Then I run on; forgetting All had past;
And my poor Sand, Eyes mixt, and gravell'd fast.
Chips, Strawes, and Feathers, Bulrushes, and Flowers,
Then take me up; and make my dayes, but Howers;   50
But as a Child, not pleas'd with any long,
To get a Rattle, these away are flung.
What shall I next? what next shall please my Eye?
For All is nothing, but Varietie;
Thus roll I Sisyphean Stones; and play
(Which he can never) all my time away.

Late by the Streame, thus did I playing Sit
With Cockle-Shells, (a Pas-time not unfitt
To my Discretion). Some, as wise as I,
Had Shittle-cockes, (and made them finely flye).   60
Another sort had Whirligigs; and Some
At Check-stones play'd, or Cherry-pit; of Foame
Others would blow a Sphære from out a Shell,
And run to catch it, like a Starre when't fell.
Thus Severally; but I, as Serious

DANIEL AND HIS BROTHER THOMAS

As any, to my Folly; Glorious
At each Encounter; and a Victorie
I priz'd, to all my Joyes Monopolie.
When in the height of All; as Shells must breake;
Mine broke; and I discountenaunct, goe seeke   70
A fresh one on the Shore; where one I found,
And hot for the Encounter, dress it round.
I washt, and Scratcht, and tooke a mightie paine
 (For it was worth All that) till not one graine
Of Sand, or Dirt, was Easy to be seene.
Not Troian Hector, in his Armour Sheene
Appear'd more Glorious, then my Champion was,
Fitt for the Lists, and I to leave the place,
Where I to such high purpose, had bene toyling;
When some kind Influence, (greived at the oft foyling   80
Of weake mortalitye) told me: I tooke
Joy, in my owne Destruction; bade me looke
To what I had bene doing; for that Mudde
I threw away, was my owne Slime; and Stood
All that remain'd, of what I valued once,
My dearest Part. Gather againe, what Chance
And Providence, are pleas'd to give; once more,
Be thy owne Keeper; from this dismall Shore
Not many doe returne.—It ceas'd; I stood
A verie Statua, dull as my owne Mudde;   90
Not Flint-wrapt Niobe, more stone did rise.
My blood was Corral; and my Breath, was Ice;
Extasied from all Sence, to thinke what low
Delusions drew me; and I knew not how;
For all the Sordid Follyes, which I sought
With Earnestnes, were now before me brought,
A Spectacle of Horror; I must breake
This marble of my Shame, my Shame to Speake.

     What can I doe (Alas)? but gather in
The little Dirt, which formerly was mine,   100
A fixed bodie; orient, and bright;

Now a foule mixture; darke, in my owne Sight;
As to my Reason, the first Chaos was.
I must goe on; Man, while he has in chase
The world, and objects vaine, looseth himselfe;
And his poor Sand, turnes wreck't into the Shelfe
Of bruitish Appetite; the Labour's over
If from this Syrte's wee our Sand recover.

Where am I now? enveloped as Deepe
To my owne wonder, as my Shame can creepe;   110
The vast Abisse, of natures unsearch't wombe
(Mother to Reason, Ignorances Tombe)
Were a prodigious Title, to enhance
My numbers weighty, and my Name advance;
This might blow up a Spirrit of that fire
Who loves to Speake, what others but Admire;
For who can Speake, what cannot be exprest?
Readers know little, and the writer Least.

Love is noe more a Ray, from that devine
Flame, then this Fish-scale, Phœbus, is from thine.   120
Tis a low bruit Affection, now which binds
In Sensuall Fetters, lowe Earth Seeking Minds;
Gold, and Desire, is Love; let minde and Face
Warme Cottages, and be the Milkmaids Grace;
Wee higher tend; Fruition of that all-
Compounded Evill is the thing wee call
Love, not improperlie. And is not witt
Worthy a name that can be Parasit?
Clawe my yong Lord, or make my Ladie smile,
With quaint Devises, worthy well her while!   130
Getting a goodly deale of patronage;
And my Lords word: *be wonder of his Age.*
Soe are they both: but Witt is growne, of Late,
Like the Trunke-hose, laught at, and out of Date;
The Drum beats loud, to fright our Villages,

Swords are the Pens, which everie Day encrease;
Our Lawes are writt in Blood; and Carv'd with Steele
Worthy the Authors. But I hope wee feele
Some ghostly Comfort yet; Religion
Has put of late, her best Apparell on;   140
And wee are all a wooeing fitt to ride,
Who should bring in this faire one, fitt for Bride.
Well; wee have tryed Enough, and rifled Each
Below the Cloaths, unto the naked breech;
And left em Soe; and soe alas they goe,
Poore Ladies, to this Day; and Like to doe.
What Age has ever yet, bene free of these?
Tis true; the last King, was a Man of Peace;
Yet fancye Quills, would note some blemish int;
And his fam'd Predecessor, though in print,   150
And painted Cloath they make her verie fine.
Yes; and her Sister, who did love to Dine
On woodcocke Christians, roasted for the nonce
With Gutts and All. Or if wee should Advance
To bugbeare Harrie whose imperious breath
Was Law enough—Oh the fine Dagger sheath!
And Codpeice of that King!—Let Nero rise
Justified, in his strange Impieties.

        Scoure of the Rust; and set an Edge on Witt.
Let each Line sparkle Courage; till wee Sitt   160
Constellated with Cæsar, in our owne,
Or others Flatterie; let Vertue (growne
Long out of use) adde some grains to the Skale
Of what wee claime to. How shall it availe?
What doe wee see applauded, everie Day?
Vice, in a vizard, goes the safest way;
The goodly masques, of Faith and Conscience
Are worne to thrive by; be't without offence,
I know none Honest; but to his owne Sight
In his owne Cause, is a Strange Hypocrite.   170

The Great Aurelius, had a flight beyond
This Region, in the Sphære of his owne mind;
And I admire his Dictates, as they are
To him selfe Precepts. What a Noble Care
It is in man, to give that Seasoning
From his owne Fountaine, shall preserve the Spring
(Through all the Ambages, of Lifes Affaire)
Backe to its liveing Source, unmixt, and Cleare!

I can be pleas'd when Lucian laughs at Witt;
And makes Philosophie, a Dizzard sitt.   180
Crack-brain'd Menippus, wisely did discerne
They taught the Things, which they would never learne.

Ime Slow in my owne Nature; Dull, and Rude;
Indifferent, in my humor; Solitude
Affects me cheifly; bashfull, have noe feat
Nor jocund humour, to ingratiate;
Yet not Averse; but rather hammer out
What I approve, then Carry mirth about.
I commend freedome; Mirth, I love, beyond
My Genius, and Adore it in my mind;   190
But cannot be Facete; some Gesture sitts
Still in my Face, which noe full mirth befitts;
And when I force it in, it comes as patt
To make me Laugh, because I know not what
I first meant should be Jeast; a thousand things
Passe, with the Garbe, when the maine Storie brings
Little to Judgement; now let me recite
Things not unworthy; and I spoyle em quite.
I have noe gracefull Meine, noe fair Accost,
Noe Foyle; Even Diamonds grow dim, in my Dust.   200

In my Discourse Ime Common; but can keepe
A trusted Secret, as the Centre deepe
Within my Bosome; I could never love
One Individuall Atome, much above

Another; I admire; to all I am
Each severall Species; for the glorious Name
Of freindship and Affection, though it draw
My Nature aptly, yet I find it rawe,
And but a Phlegme, where I would most expresse:
Now tis a Flame within me; and I lesse   210
Consider my owne Interest, then the Claime
Another has unto me, in that Name.

    Now whether Education, or what else
I doe not know; perhaps from principles
Of Constitution, some unwonted Awe,
Something, under what Name, I doe not know,
Strikes me, in Majestie; and though I praise
All Government, as Government; I raise
My Selfe, with more Delight, to looke upon
A monarchs Scepter, then the Axe, or Gowne.   220

    This when I wondring fixe at; I behold
Our Royall Master, in Afflictions old;
But vig'orous, in vertue; and Dispred
In all his Princelie Rayes; not hindered
As the Eclipsed Sun, by the moons dull
Hydropticke bodie, to obscure him full;
But Charles, whose more illustrious Beams strike throw'
The giddie planet, that the world may know
Tis but her Errant motion; Hee, the Same
Light to the world; Health and Life-bringing Flame: 230
Soe Father Saturne, by his Sawcie Son
Seaven yeare agoe, was interpos'd. Tis Runne
I hope out, in our Iland; Meteors must
After a while, burne out, and dye ith' Dust:
But the great Luminaries carrie Flame
T'enrich the world, and make it worth a Name.

    Freedome, and love of Truth, is all I boast;
I know but little. Hee that knowes the most

Is not an Inch beyond me; I can Sitt
Pleased in my owne; Hee's plunged in his witt;   240
For Knowledge is a Quicksand; where wee can
Not free our selves, till wee the burthen, Man,
Devest; our Flesh, the Scales which doe obscure
Our Intellectuall Eyes, and Death's the Cure.
Then chang'd, wee move, another Nature; See
And know things trulie, as they truly bee
In their owne Causes; till when, wee pursue
A Wildgoose-Chase, to what none ever knew;
Hee that knew All, knew nothing; or at least
Knew, all Hee knew was Follie with the rest.   250

     Then bring me wine; Call in the merrie Crue;
Let petty Sphæres their heightened Peggs up-Scrue
To rivall, with the greater; and disperse
Our frolicke Joyes, to all the universe.
Soe Poets are themselves; let Dulnes Sitt
On the dry brow; wee live in mirth and witt;
Be sprightly, as the morne; Anticipate
Time, in his motion; and Astonish Fate
To make our owne; While the dull Sisters winke
And passe our Threds, Halfe-drunke, to see us Drink.   260

     Are there noe Females in the house? come in
Coy Modesties, where have you Absent bene?
From what, your Wishes rectified, prefer
To our Desires. A Day, has bene a Yeare;
Strike up a louder Note while wee advance
Preparatoryes, to our Daliance.

     Me thinkes, againe I thirst; Swell me a Boule
Lesse Emptie then the Ayre. Let Misers howle
At their slow Incomes; tis a Noble prize
To laugh at fortune, and the world despise.   270

     This hideous Peice of madnes, has perchance
Ith' Scæne, less Envie, and lesse Arrogance

     . 8 .

Then some wee call Discretions; perhaps lesse
Impietie; but Sin, who can Expresse?
Til all within us; and our Thoughts scarce know
What tis wee would, or what wee would not Doe.
Soe then wee whine, upon our Errors past,
And Swimme our Brains in Follye to the Last.

Our Fancies are our Follies; and our Boast
Is all our Crime; Strange Paradox! almost   280
To Stifle Reason; yet it is most true.
I've found it, in my Selfe; and Soe may You.

Ut Surgam Cado

Munitus, et clausus, contra externa,
intra me maneo;
a curis omnibus Securus,
Præter unam,
ut fractum, Subactumq: hunc animum,
rectæ Rationi, ac Deo Subiiciam;
et animo,
cœteras res humanas.

A VINDICATION OF POESIE

TRUTH SPEAKES of old, the Power of Poesie;
Amphion, Orpheus, Stones, and Trees, could move;
Men first by verse, were taught Civilitie;
Tis knowne, and granted; yet would it behove
    Mee, with the Ancient Singers, here to Crowne
    Some later Quills, Some Makers of our owne.

Who has not heard, Mæonides loud Straine?
Macedons Envie? who did never yet
(That has of Numbers heard; but) heare againe
The Ascrean Pipe? or great Musæus witt?   10
    Who has not heard of Heroes, Demigods?
    Of Centaur's? Cyclop's? Sacred Founts, and woods?

See antique Rome; and though, you see her plaine
In honest Ennius; can you but admire
Pious Æneas? or the Mantuan
As Sweet in feilds, as statelie in Troies fire?
    Not Euxine Pontus, nor the Tirants Lust
    Shall make Fame be less glorious, Fate, lesse Just;

For after Death, dyes Envye; all men find
Honour, due to their merits; this, he taught;   20
And this, he found. Live Ovid (unconfin'd)
To better mention; beyond a Thought
    Of *o cur vidi;* never more exclaime:
    Hee wrong'd his owne, and added to thy Name.

Loe yet another; he who has not heard
Pharsalia's Trumpet, never knew his Fate;
Cordubaes Glorie; see the Poet smear'd
In guiltles Blood, triumph in Neroes hate.
    His Name shall live; and he, that cannot raise
    A verse to Lucan, dye without his praise.   30

A noble Store, doth Italie produce,
Which hap'lie may advance, their fame as great;
Danazar, Petrarch, Tassoes honored Muse;
Swift Arne, the Thuscan Soile, noe more shall beat,
    Nor Swan-clad Po run Sweet, nor fame be Just
    If Dant forgotten be, or Ariost':

Nor shall the Muse, of that French Eagle dye,
Devine Sire Bartas; and the happie writt
Of Bellay, here shall live eternallie,
Eternizing his Name, in his owne Witt.   **40**
    From hence, by a Short passage, wee are come
    To veiw the Treasure, of our witts at home.

I am not bound to honour Antique names;
Nor am I led, by other Men, to Chuse
Any thing worthy, which my judgment blames.
Heare better Straines, though by a later Muse:
    The Sweet Arcadian Singer, first did raise
    Our Language Current, and deserved his Baies;

That Lord of Pen'herst; Pen'herst whose sad walls
Yet mourne their Master, in the Belgicke fray   **50**
Untimelie lost; to whose deare Funeralls
The Medwaie doth its constant Tribute paye;
    But glorious Pen'herst, Medwaies waters once
    With Mincius shall, and Mergeline advance.

The Shepherds Boy; best knowen by that Name
Colin; upon his homely oaten Reed
With Roman Titirus may share in Fame;
But when a higher path, hee seem's to tread,
    He is my wonder; for who yet has seene
    Soe Cleare a Poeme, as his Faierie Queene?   **60**

The Sweetest Swan of Avon; to the faire
And Cruel Delia, passionatelie Sings;

Other mens weaknesses, and follies, are
Honour and witt in him; each Accent brings
 A Sprig to Crowne him Poet; and Contrive
 A Monument, in his owne worke to live.

Draiton is sweet, and Smooth; though not exact
Perhaps, to stricter Eyes; yet he shall live
Beyond their Malice. To the Sceane and Act,
Read Comicke Shakespeare; or if you would give   70
 Praise, to a Just Desert, crowning the Stage,
 See Beaumont, once the honour of his Age.

The reverent Donne, whose quill soe purely fil'd,
Lives to his Character; & though he claime
A greater glory, may not be exil'd
This Commonwealth; the entrance of his fame
 Thus as the Sun, to either Hemisphere
 Still the same Light; Hee moved with us here.

But as a Poet; all the softnesses,
The Shadow, Light, the Ayre, & Life of Love;   80
The Sharpnes of all Witt; ev'n bitternes
Makes Satire Sweet; all wit did soe emprove.
 'Twas flamed in him, 'Twas but warm upon
 His Embers; He was more; & yet is Donne.

Here pause a little; for I would not Cloy
The curious Eare, with recitations;
And meerly looke at names; attend with Joy
Unto an English Quill, who rivall'd once
 Rome, not to make her blush; and knowne of late
 Unenvied ('cause unequall'd) Laureate.   90

This, this was Jonson; who in his owne name
Carries his praise; and may he shine alone;

73 soe purely] Ms.; God purely Grosart.
73-84 These lines are added in the margin of the Ms. in a different hand.
82 soe emprove] Ms.; God emprove Grosart.

I am not tyed, to any generall Fame,
Nor fixed by the Approbation
    Of great ones; But I Speake without pretence;
    Hee was, of English Dramatickes, the Prince.

Be glad, illiterate English, that ye may
Heare Lucan, in your best of Language speake;
Lucan, the mouth of Story; Sung by Maye,
To yet his owne; his owne, soe truly like   100
    The Roman Genius, as yow cannot say,
    This was by Lucan done, or yet by Maye.

Let Naso sing his best; and once lament
That best, did want his last life-giving hand;
His works, our Sands; though not in banishment
A Stranger, in a wild & remote Land,
    Has polisht out, & imp's his wing, to flye
    Beyond Rome's Eagles, & her Emperye.

Now leaves he there; but as he had Disdaignd
Her witt, or Empire, confind to his reach;   110
The holy Ground he treads; which though they gaind,
They never got; he did; & now doth teach
    To us dull Ilanders; the inspired Layes
    Which David sung; & which the Preacher sayes.

The noble Overburies Quill, has left
A better wife, then he could ever find;
I will not search too deep, lest I should lift
Dust from the dead; Strange power of womankind,
    To raise and ruine; for all he will claime,
    Is from that Sex; his Birth, his Death, His Fame.   120

But I spin out to long; let me draw up
My thred, to honour Names of my owne time

97-114   These lines are added in the margin of the Ms. in a different hand.
  105   banishment]; banisment Ms.

Without their Eulogies, for it may Stop
With Circumstantiall Termes, a wearie Rhime;
 Suffice it if I name em; that for me
 Shall stand, not to refuse their Eulogie;

The noble Falkland, Digbie, Carew, Maine,
Beaumond, Sand's, Randolph, Allen, Rutter, May,
The Devine Herbert, and the Fletchers twaine,
Habinton, Shirley, Stapilton; I Stay   130
 Too much on names; yet may I not forget
 Davenant, and Suckling, eminent in witt.

Waller not wants the glory of his verse;
And meets a noble praise, in every Line;
What should I adde in honour? to reherse
Admired Cleaveland? by a verse of mine?
 Or give the glorious Muse of Denham praise?
 Soe with'ring Brambles stand, to liveing Bayes.

These may suffice; not only to advance
Our English honour, but for ever crowne   140
Poesie, 'bove the reach of Ignorance.
Only dull fooles unmoved, admire their owne
 Stupiditie; and all beyond their Sphere
 Is Madnes, and but tingling in the Eare.

Great Flame Whose raies at once, have power to peirce
The frosted Skull of Ignorance, and Close
The mouth of Envie; if I bring a verse
Unapt to move; my admiration Flowes
 With humble Love, and Zeale in the intent
 To a Cleare Rapture, from the Argument. 150

133-138 These lines are added in the margin of the Ms. in a different hand.

To time and honour

Faire Albion, of the world, thou fairest Ile!
And thou Deare Yorkshire, thou my native Soyle,
My Nurse, my Mother! Oh, how can I pay
My Gratitude? Muse! teach me what to Say;
How shall I praise thee most? let me looke backe
To former Ages, and I heare em Speake
With almost wonder; what prodigious name
Can boast he Saw, he went, and overcame
Further then Some of ours? Third Edwards Son,
Son of brave Sire! how did he over run   10
The face of France? and Victorie Create
In his owne fortune; pardon, if I say't:
Hee was not Second, to those names wee heare
Pronounc'd with Admiration, and Feare.
Not that Great Alexander, nor the Name
Of Punicke Hannibal, nor Caesars Fame
Outshine his Glories; had he seene a Day
As large in Time, he'd beene as great as they.
Him Shall I praise? or his brave father most?
Or his great Grandsire? or of Richard boast,   20
That Richard Lions-heart; and from that Stemme
Bring downe the Glorie to fifth Harries name,
Or the fowerth Edward; these and many more
(Though not in Fame) in Blood inferior
Might I repeat; but better let them goe
To swell huge Chronicle in Folio.
How shall I praise thee most? in thy full peace!
Thy nat'rall Bounties, and the large increase
Which everie yeare forth brings; thy inborne wealth
Thy selfe existence, where wee need noe Stealth   30
Of Marchants to enrich us; but might rest
Safe in our Selves, with native bounties blest.
Shall I praise one, or All? for All are thine?

Noe more will I admire, the Southerne Shine
Nor Easterne perfumes, nor the wealth o th' west;
But thinke thee fairest, Sweetest, richest, Best;
Forgetting Chaucer, and Dan Lidgates Rhime,
Loe here, the Glorie, of our modern time,
A learned Age. Since great Elizaes reigne
And Peace came in; the proud Italian,   40
And justly proud in Poesie, will allow
The English (though not Equall) next him now.
The noble Sidney crown'd with liveing Bayes;
And Spencer cheif, (if a peculear praise
May pass, and from the rest not derogate)
The learned Jonson, whose Dramaticke State
Shall stand admir'd Example, to reduce
Things proper, to the light, or buskind Muse.
Many the present Age afford, of which
Heare Falkland, Digbie, Beaumond, Carew, rich   50
In their Composures Severall; with whom
Maye, Allein, Randolph, Shirley, Rutter come;
Sons of thy wombe all these; with whom may I
(Though in a weake, and humble Poesie)
Thy glories Celebrate, and quitt the Score
Nature obligeth me. I aske noe more;
Not that I covet fame; let those high names
Inherite all the Glorie, of their Thames,
And live to many ages, though I fall
In scorned Dust, and have noe name at all.   60
Suffice it I may sing upon thy flood,
Neglected Humber; or my Muse (less proud)
Sport in the Sedges, of my neighbouring Streame,
Poore as my verse, neither deserving name;
And may the village where I had my birth
Enclose as Due, my Bodie in her Earth.

50 rich] Ms.; Rich, Grosart. Here Grosart's misreading makes of the
word *rich* the name of a poet.

A PASTORALL ODE
THE EGLOGUE IS LOST

COME LEAVE the Cities Strife
And chuse a Countrie Life.
There place my Joyes; and let my wandring mind
Be fixt, and there confined;
There, with my loved Sheepe
And my owne Silvia, I as prince can keepe,
Crowned Monarch, in her Brest,
Equall loving, equall Blest.
Come, Come away my thoughts, be fixed here,
For greater pleasures, have the greater Care.   10

What though I doe not find,
My Galleries, there Lined
With Atticke hangings, nor Corinthian Plate
(Ensignes of greater State
Placed for more ornament)
Is't in these vanities, to find Content?
I doe not Covet these;
An humble Roofe, may please
An humble mind; and who can tell? there may
Be troubled Thoughts in Downe, as well as Hay.   20

Though Gray or Russet be
My height of Gayetie,
Though I nor Plush, nor gaudie Sattin have
Enough; I doe none Crave.
What though, my Backe, or Thigh,
Not Cloathed be with Woole, in Tirian Dye!
Nor Beavers Fleece enrich
My Browes! tis not the Itch
Of Glorie takes me; I can often find
In Garments trimme, a Discomposed Mind.   30

The Colchian Bird's to mee
Noe Baite of Luxurie;
Nor doe I seeke, th' Ionian Partridge more
Then Hens, from my owne Doore;
The Lushious oyster is,
And Lobster, though of treeble price
-Not moveing; neither seeke
I Spanish wines, or Greeke
To Stirre my Spirrite; I can gladly bee
Sated with lesse, and Shun the Luxurie.   40

What tho' perhaps I want
Beauties, and have noe hant
Where I may wanton, and quench lustful **fires;**
Noe need; for those desires
I doe not harbour. Soe
I flye the Sin, and the occasion too;
For Silvia is to me
More then varietie;
In her deare Eyes I joy, and can take **thence**
A Flame, or Modestie, and Innocence.   50

Noe Lustfull Raptures me
Hold in Captivitie.
I seeke noe wanton Mistress; I can **Spend**
(And wish time might not End)
Daies, and Years, with Silvia;
Shee, to my pleased Thoughts, is more then **they**
Can fancie, in their Dreams.
I would, these foule extreames,
Not less then Scylla, or Charibdis **Shun;**
There is an Isthmus, I would fixe upon.   60

The gaudie Cities pride,
Nor what they boast beside,
Nor their full Treasures, nor their furnisht roomes

DANIEL IN HORATIAN COSTUME

Where Silken Madam comes;
Not all the Cloath's they weare
Nor their high feastings, and luxurious fare;
Not Madam's selfe, can make
Mee, countrie Life forsake.
Noe; let them riot, revel, feast, and vant
Their garments rich as these; the Sin I want.   70

Ile shun Court Care, and the proud Cities Strife,
Center my Joyes, in a poore Countrie Life.

THE SPRING

Now the Springe enters; now the Sun doth Cheare
The quick'ned Earth; and trees by Cold made bare
Now gin to bud; the Earth doth now begin
To flourish, in her Sweet and glorious Trimne;
The Silver Stream's, bound up by winters Cold,
Glide fairly, where they murmured of old.
The goodly Meadowes, russet late, and Dead,
In a fresh Dresse, are now apparelled;
The mountaine tops are bared, and where the Snow
Late covered, the Spring begins to Shew.   10
Thither the Lads, dull'd with the winters rest,
To joy in wonted Sports, doe gladly hast;
Now Joyes the Industrious Bee, and the Ant now
(Embleme of Providence) her selfe doth Show,
Warme in her winters Store; doth now againe
Labour, and make provision, to sustaine
Her little bodie, for the after day;
Now flyes the Maggot, in her paintings gay
(Signe of faire weather) and doth now invite
Decrepit years, to tast the Springs delight.   20
I will not call the Cuckooe, with the Spring;

(Unnaturall foolish Bird) let her voyce ringe
T'affright the Citie, and an omen carrie
Of Fate, to fooles, and old men, when they marrie;
But here the Redbrest, and gray Linnets Singe;
The poore wren, flutters with an Eager wing
To gaine yond' highest Sprig, and there doth pay
A Ceremonious Himne, to welcome day;
Whilst from that Grove, the haples Philomel
Sweetly, though Sadly, doth her Storie tell;   30
The little Dazies, shake their Deawie Lock's;
The ambitious woodbine climbs againe, and mocks
The tardie Gilliflower; the lillye in
Her liveing Robe, of Innocence, doth Shine;
For those of Cost, and Art, to me are poor.
Nature is Rich, and Curious in her Store;
And this same Marigold, or violet here
To the transplanted Tulip, I preferre;
Loe where the Larke, borne on her active wing,
Pouers forth her Song of Joy, unto the Spring;   40
Lamb's joyous friske, and play now each with other,
Neglect the Teate, and leave the Ewe, their mother.
Inspired with the Time, may my Muse frame
Notes, with the Larke, be Sportive with the Lambe.

WOMAN CHARACTRED

CHAST, AS AN AGED HEREMIT, at his Death;
Faire, as the morning, sweeter then the Breath
Of Violets; and as the Turtle, true
Where She affects, never enquiring new;
And (seing the world 'counts it an ornament)
She Shall be rich, sufficient to Content;
Not Starrs, but equall Sunn's, are her faire Eyes,
Dressing the Sphere, where all perfection Lyes;
Soe sweetly modest, as in Either Eye
(Without a guide) men might read Chastitie;   10
The common Praise, of Lillie, and the Rose
Fresh as in June, here in December growes;
Her necke, her brest, her wast; (for lower, I
Not dare to fall) might ravish everie Eye;
To adorne these, Motion, which in soe faire state
Shee doth Expresse, Juno might imitate;
Sober, to speake, but when her Accents come,
Minerva present, would be stricken dumbe;
A Mind, beyond Expression; vertuous, more
Then Anchorites, even in their Dying Hower: 20
All these, in Woman; but which, which is Shee?
All women, are soe; or at least, should Bee.

SILVIA REVOLTED

WHEN I, unto the fameles Devia, now
Utter my song, the emptie winds disperse
My Laboured Numbers, and let noe man know
Their Sound. Ah! there have I, in mightie verse
Had better Audience, of my fellow peeres;
The proud Amintas, did not scorne to bow
    And give Attention; nor disdaine to joyne
    His verses, with the notes which then were mine.

When hee, the bright Urbana, magnified;
And I my Silvia sung, in Equall Sound;   10
Silvia, the fairest, mortall ever Eyed;
But ah! my greife! there is my hearts great wound.
Silvia, whom once I almost Deified,
Revolted is; and newer Loves hath found.
    Ah faithles Silvia; whether shall I flye
    For Passion to enrage my Poesie?

Whither! but to the Eyes, of Silvia false?
And dash my bitter Inke, against their shine;
Defame that glorious feature, which exalts
Her name to wonder, in some verse of mine;   20
Crie recreant, and recall, what ever calls
Her faire, or worthy. Draw another Line
    And what I said, unsay; or shall I keepe
    In modest limits? and let Passion Sleepe?

I will not wrong her Name, which gave mine Life,
In a Cleare Mention; She to whom I sung
A Thousand Sonnets, and brought Numbers rife,
To Celebrate her Glories; She who hung
My browes with virgin Chaplets; never greife
Shall Blind my Judgment, with soe foule a wrong;   30
    But Silvia, in my verse, shall keepe a Seat,
    Though me, she Scorne, and happilie forget.

Though me She Scorne; and give her love away
To proud Penandro; and the guiltie Crue
Rivall her favours; I may see a Day
She will be glad to grace my love anew;
Meanwhile, in Libertie, I will Assay
My fancie (taught by her) and reaccrue
    My Thoughts into their Station; and then Scorne
    Her faith retracted, old, and overworne.   40

Scorne Returned

Are you the only faire? false Silvia? noe;
    Twas I, that gave the lustre to your Eyes;
And sung your Beauties greater farre & moe
    Then Nature gave; or all the flatteries
Of your deluding Glasse, could ever Show.
        I placed a liveing Rose
      On either Cheeke; and drest
        Those Lipps faire, which disclose
      Pearles, in their liveing nest;
I drest, with polish't Ivorie, that brow,   10
And to your lockes put all the Sorceries
    Of Nature; 'twas I, brought
All perfect Lineaments, unto your Frame;
    And in huge Numbers taught
A Character of Beautie, in your Name.
    Then are you fond, to flye your owne desert;
And your neglect, may bring my Love to Scorne;
    Ile chuse another, who in everie part
Shall have more Sweets; farewell, Oh false forsworne.
    Ile bring an Æthiope, and with small endeavour   20
    Raise better feature there, then you had ever.

SUPPLANTED

DISLOYALL SILVIA; See
What now your Scorne has done.
I have my Libertye,
Goe follow you your owne.
I sing another Name, and sing her faire;
Loe where she Comes, with thousand Cupids sett
In either Eye; and all the Sweets, which werre
Your beauties prize, in her againe are mett;
You were but what I sung you; when I call
My verses backe, your Beauties vanish All.   10

See; (to torment your soule)
Who has tooke up, your place.
I must Confesse, a foule
Deformed, Sootie face;
Darke as the Night, her Eyes; her haire undrest
Like Adders, on her Curbed Shoulders fall;
Her Limnes Distorted; and her name profest,
Leud Prostitute to Everie Strangers call;
Yet, in a liveing verse, I will transforme
Her faults, perfection, and her name adorne.   20

Splitt your proud heart with greife,
To know, another must
Gaine, by my verse, a Life;
When yours, hid in the rust
Of Sad Decay, noe mention shall find.
My deare Nicotiana is more true
And not soe Common; (though with every wind
She varie Love) and Fairer much then you;
This Common Strumpet, of the Times, to you
Is Faire, and Chast, and (though still changeing) true.   30

To Nicotiana
A RAPTURE

COME MY NICOTIANA; weele renew
Our free delights, and Appetite pursue.
Wee fearles will enjoy those reall Joyes
Lovers would paint, in their fantasticke toyes;
And boldly Justifie, what wee have done,
Though thousand Curious Eyes, were looking on.
    Come; with a hundred Blandishments weele trye
Strange Subtleties, in Loves great Misterie;
In varied formes, thy pliant Limbes shall cast
Their knots, at once, about my necke and wast;   10
Thy poudred Tresses, over mine shall spread
And strangelye mixt, make it but all one head;
Close as the power of Love can Joyne us, then
Wee will new Joyes invent; such as the Pen
Of wanton Poets pussle; my free hand
Noe bashfull blush, shall ever Countermand;
But in a Thousand formes, thy Tresses part
And slide along with uncontrolled Art
Thy daintie Bodie, not to fear a frowne
For soyling, of thy new white Sattin Gowne.   20
My willing Lips shall part, to catch thy Breath,
Sweet, as the Hony-deaw, which Hybla hath.
There will I hang; and all my veins inspire
With Ardent Wishes taken from thy fire;
Hard on my Lips, thy wanton tongue, shall press,
And by new Chimistrie, in Wantonnes,
Send the rich Quintessence, of all I seeke,
In Dalliance through that faire Alimbecke;
There will I sucke with Cunning Industrie
Thy Spirrits Extracted, by loves Alekimie.   30
When we are be-qualm'd, that long imbraces has
Made dull Desire, and wee shall only passe
Faint breathings, I will summon a fresh Store

Of Vigour, farre more Active then before;
And with neat Tittillations, new provoke
Decaied fire in thee, to the full Stocke;
Invent new postures; & outdoe the old
Fictions, to make em Storie; when with bold
Uncurbed flames, wee grapple; and not part,
But to renew our Action, and our Art.   40
      Let fooles be modest; and the novice say
Hee did the Act, where noe Eye could betray;
Such pettie fears, our generous Thoughts despise;
Our pleasure is made rich, by many Eyes;
And with an Equall glorie, wee dare vye
In Artfull Sleights, to all the Standersby.
Such Confidence, is Manly; doth appeare
Worthy all Titles, wee can glorie here.
Thus, my Nicotiana, wee will move,
Careles who see; fearles who know our Love.   50

An epode

Farre from the Citties Strife; as far from fame,
      I wish, to keepe my name;
Careles of popular vote, or vaine Applause
      To mine, though for Just Cause;
Let the bright Inke, which Phebus doth distill,
      Through everie Noble Quill,
Run in a Clearer path. Had I bene borne
      Below my fate, the Scorne
Of other Men; and had noe more extract
      Then what my selfe could Act;   10
Yet in this obscure fortune, had I ben
      Capable of a Pen,
I would have Squared a way, for my owne verse,
      As void of vulgar fears,
As overborn by Selfe opinion.
      I would have made my owne

Judgment an Equall Arbiter, to Define
    The worth of everie Line;
And let Fastidious Censures of the Times
    Guild loose and borrowed Rhimes;   20
Such, who or want, or what they have, betray
    To the most Sordid way
Of Ignorance; such as affect the vote
    Of Stentor-follies Throte;
Or ravil out the Loome, of all their witt
    To play Court-Parasit':
These waies I hate, and Scorne; if what I penn'd
    Fell to soe base an End,
My guiltye Quill would splitt; my Inke would rise
    Into my face, and Eyes;   30
Judge Great Apollo! if I have done ought
    With a presumptuous Thought
That any name, could make my numbers flye,
    Beyond their Poesie.
To noe Collossus, could I ever bend;
    Or at the Court attend
With my owne Sin, and Follie in a Sheet;
    To prostrate, at the feet
Of painted greatnes. Not a Lord, one drop
    Of my Just Inke, shall hope   40
Beyond his Merit; I dare not abuse
    Soe much, my freeborne Muse,
But utter Truth; it is not in their Fate
    To raise, nor Terminate
A true Composure. Wee admire the Good
    Without Alloy of Blood,
And Justly praise them, beyond all the Date
    Of Brass, or marble State.
Wee adde to them, if Either, and doe give
    Their Vertues breath, to live   50
In Mention; and the honour of one Name
    Shall nere be old, with Fame.
But tis Enough; I hate a Servitude
Either to Might, or to the Multitude.

To the Memorie of the Best Dramaticke English Poet Ben: Jonson: 1638

GREAT FLAME of English Poets gon! how shall
Wee strew our flowers, at thy Funerall?
What obsequies performe! What rites prepare
Unto thy Herse? what monument, but were
Too narrów to Containe Thee! or what State
But were beneath the honour of thy fate?
Noe, rather; wee (remaining of the Tribe,
Sad orphans) can but wish, what wee ascribe
Unto thy Merit; all wee bring to thee,
Is but our Tears; our filial Pietie.   10
      Great Lord of Arts! and Father of the Age,
The first, and best Informer of the Stage!
How shall wee speake of him? what Numbers bring
T' empassionate? and worthy orgies Sing?
What shall wee Say? Shall wee in a Just Zeale
Rebuke the Age of Ignorane, and tell
Aloud his Merits? shall wee weepe, or boast
His worth? or Losse? shall wee say, when wee lost
Him, a sad Night of follie did orespread
This Iland, as wee see; and wee are dead   20
Rather then Hee wee weep for? for Hee, still
Lives to instruct the Age, with a Strong Quill.
And as he did, from Ignorance, reduce
Th' abused Stage; Soe has he left to us
(Who act upon this greater Theatre)
Grave morall Pandects; Strong, & yet soe Cleare
Hee is his owne Expositor; and wee
(If sottishly not blind or worse) may see
Vertue in Act; and everie gracefull Step
She treads may be our Path; but wee all Sleepe   30
Uncapable of what Hee taught; or how

To valew what Hee left us. I could bow
(And would the Age, might doo't without offence)
To name him, with a Modest Reverence;
For Shall wee kneele to Titles? and observe
Formalities? to those, who nought deserve
(More then their name, or painted outside give)
And shall My Lord, have a prerogative
For vertue in his Ancestors? (though hee
Perhaps the Shame, of all his Pedigree)   40
And our Great Lord of witt; where vertue in
Her Sphere did move; where Art and Judgment Shine,
Inseparable bee, with Common Men
And vulgar Mention names? Oh! the Pen
Of Witt, and Truth forbid it; rather let
The worthles present Age, his name forget;
For wee are Emulous fooles; and will admitt
Noe Rivalls, in the Claime wee lay to witt.
     But After-Ages, (more Judicious,
Unswaied by Passion, only Sedulous   50
To honour vertue) shall, (I will not Doubt)
Advance his name; when the despised Rout
(His Scorne) shall perish, in the filthy Smoake
Of their owne Follies; then all Eyes shall looke
With Joy and Admiration, to receive
A Light their Fathers could not. I will leave
Only this little: Judgment shall Allow,
(When Men, have Eyes, to see; & witt to know
Who merit most) the greatest Eulogie
For Language, Art, and all Dexteritie   60
Of Witt, to Him; and happ'lie were the flame
Extinct, wee might recover't in his name:
A Charme soe stronge, Who ever shall reherse
Ben: Jonson, cannot chuse but make a verse.

Upon ben jonsons booke

Bee not Deceived (Dull world) Hee is not Dead;
Rumor is false; open His Booke and read;
It is Himselfe; there, Everie Scene affords
Words above Action; Matter beyond words;
If Readers, what I say will not suffice
T' evince your Follies; I dare bid you twice,
What yet you have not Done: Open, and Read;
Recant; or else tis You, not Hee that's Dead.

The dedication of a poem, now lost; written in the royall expedition against the scotts

TO THE KING:

All fitt to serve you, in this great Designe,
Where Action fires brave minds, to entertaine
Bright hopes of honour: and your Subject stand
A Guard to you; a Glorie to your Land;
Where Armes are only usefull: Sir, excuse
(When now Bellona thunders) a Sad Muse,
Who can noe other way, her Tribute bring,
But a weake forme of words; the offering
Of a neglected Poet, who to Fame,
Bequeath's his Numbers, rich in your great Name;   10
Tho' Sir; if I were happie, this might live
A Time, beyond what all your Annalls give:
And when the brasen Trumpe of Historie
Shall splitt with Time; and to Posteritie
Give scarce the Names, of your dead Ancestors;
When Statues, monuments, and high rear'd Towers
Shall drop to Dust, and lye forgotten in
A heape of Ruines; when the mouth of Sin

Shall spitt upon Just vertues, and deface
The Light of Truth, and Majestie disgrace;   20
When all the world shall suffer, in her Jawes
Wee stand Secure, and doe not feare the Lawes
Of Surly fate, nor the Decrees of Time;
Confident, in the force, of mighty Rhime.
     But Franticke Poets erre; tis you can give
A Life to verse; the great Prerogative
Of Numbers cannot stand, without the Breath
Of Majestie; that only frees from Death;
Creates a Poet; and gives verse her wings.
This Sir: wee know; and thus this Poet Sings.   30

THIS WAS PLACED IN THE END
OF THE SAME POEM:

TO THE KING:

THUS Sr: againe I kneele; may heaven blesse
Your high Designes, with Glorie and Successe;
May victorie Attend you; but how low
Imperfect Wishes fall to what wee owe?
May you be great, and Happie; and Survive
Glorious to Fame; that Poets may derive
(Poets long Ages hence) from your great Name
All their Invention, all their Art, their Flame.
I need not wish (what Heaven ordains) the Glorie
Immortall, when y' have past this Transitorie;   10
I would not live to See the Change; though once
I know it must. Long, long 'bove fate or Chance
May you reigne here; and then I wish as much
Glorie, as Immortalitie can touch.
     Enough; and if these Accents strike your Ears
With the least pleasure; I will bring a verse
To your Great Name, shall be an Emulation
To all the haughtie Poets, of your Nation.

My hopes live in your Breath; and to your Eyes
My Numbers fall; the Poet lives, or Dies,   20
As you pronounce. Sir: you may raise a Name
From obscure Nothing, to the Best of Fame;
A Name in nothing happie, but to Sing
The Glories of soe Great, soe Good a King.

ONE DESIRING ME TO READ, BUT SLEPT IT OUT; WAKENING

NAY; DOE NOT SMILE; my Lips shall rather dwell
                    For ever on my Pipe,
Then read to you one word, or Sillable:
                    You are not ripe
            To Judge, or Apprehend
            Of witt. Ile rather Spend
Six howers together, in Tobacco-taking
Then read to you, and cannot keep you wakeing.

ÆNIGMA

A CRABBED STUMPE; yet Sillie Husbands Care
 (Too much Indulgent, to the great impaire
Of his more profitable Howers) did dresse
And manure it; more valewing encrease
From this unhopefull Impe, then all the Store
Hee had beside; and he had many more;
And what his Art, or Industrie, could bring
To make it fresh, he did, in everie Thing.
Still was it Seir; noe Leafe would ever peepe
Or Blossome Spread; but Nature as asleepe   10
Continued in the Trunke. The Husband (wed
To his first undertakings) Cherished

The hopeles Stocke, with more then common Care;
And to a better Soyle, and better Ayre
Transplanted it; yet could he gather small
Or little Hopes, that it should beare at All;
Only a liveing Sap, it did retaine,
Without all verdure. Thus it did remaine
Thrice Seaven Summers; without any Show
To repay his great Care; at last one Bough   20
Without or Leafe, or Blossome did produce
A Fruite of bitter, and unsavorie Juice.
Some who did tast it, wormewood would compare
Unto its relish; and some others Sweare
Henbane had lesse of venome; for in Strange
Tumors it blisterd; and the blood did range
With an unwonted Heate, and violence
Through the infected Bodies; such offence
Came in its first production; still the fond
Artificer, would hope Something beyond;   30
Though the Cheife Gard'ner, would have had it cast
Into the Fire, or throwne out with the wast.
Hee with a Cultivating Hand, doth give
It all the Rites; for which perhaps, in five,
Sixe, or Seaven yeare (though Leafe, nor other green
It ever had the least) there has bene Seene
Some fruite; which I in Curiositie
Once tasted. Tis a harsh one, and a Drie;
Worse then a Medler; but more Calme, more Safe
Unto the Palat, then the first by th' halfe.   40
Loe here, the Issue of his hopes, and now
Againe it is declin'd; for such as know
Fruit by appearance, thinke the last years fruite
Deadlie Aconite; and in the root
Some say a Canker lyes; to gnaw and wast
The tree, unverdant from the first, to the last;
Nor is it Strange (and take the Sence togither)
The Thing, which never flourished, should Wither.

43-44 fruite / Deadlie Aconite;]; fruite, / Deadlie, a Aconite; **Ms.**

Fame

Mortall, wouldst thou wooe a Feature
   In a glasse? or please thy Eye
With a Shadow, for a Creature?
   Or bring all thy hopes, to Dye
In the Earlie Spring of Nature
   For a breath of vanitie?
Or resigne, what you may claime
To the vogue of vulgar Fame?

Quickly Come; and here behold
   The Strange Mirror: she presents 10
Earth, and Ashes; Seeming Gold
   To enrich your Monuments;
Frees from Envie, keeps from old
   The feature of your faire intents;
Publisheth, in liveing Storie
All that can adde, to your Glorie.

Would you be thought rich, or wise?
   Valiant? or be ever yong?
Handsome? nothing Shee denies
   That has being, from the Tongue. 20
Were you odious, for your vice,
   Infamous, as could be Sung,
Time should keepe your monument
Vertue's liveing ornament;

But noe more; let Sence retire,
   And with Reasons Eye, Survay
The vast Shadow you admire.
   Waneing, wasting with the Day;
Time is false, and Fame a Liar;
   Vertue, only fixt; and may 30
Create, beyond the breath of fame,
A Thousand Honours to your Name.

Agonie

Oh I am Cold; the wombe of Earth may thaw
My frost; not waters in their Current draw
      Such Chillnes; I am Cold
As the Sad house of winter; or the Feet
Of Rocks, involved where the waters meet;
      And yet I am not old.

Oh I am Sad; as virgins, when they loose
Their pregnant hopes of him, they meant for Spouse;
      Or widdowes in their Fate;
Sad, as a Parent, for his hopefull Heire;   10
Or as a Prince, deprived of Crowne, and Chaire;
      Yet hardly know for what.

Oh I am wounded; deeply strucke, and beare
The fatall Javeline, with me everie where;
      Into the marrow thrilled;
A Thousand Dolours, now assaile my hart,
Of which, Alcides hardly knew a part;
      And yet I am not kill'd.

Oh I am Sicke; as women in their throes
Or men in rageing feavers; to my woes   20
      The Gout, and Stone are Ease;
Fire in my Brest; and Poison fills my veins;
Bane in my Breath; and Frensie in my brains;
      Yet know not my Disease.

Oh I am Dead; if it be death, to dwell
In Shades of night, in mansions next to Hell;
      In fear's, and Miserie;
In Darknes, where noe hope of Light can enter,
In greifs unpittied, as though in the Center;
      And yet I cannot Dye.   30

An essay

ENDEVOURING TO ENNOBLE OUR ENGLISH POESIE
BY EVIDENCE OF LATTER QUILLS;
AND REJECTING THE FORMER

SHALL I BE onlye Hereticke in witt?
Forbid Appolloe; rather let me Splitt
My lab'ring Quill to Death. Noe; when I first
Enterd a Poet, Modestie, (the worst
Companion of Sedition) brought me on
In tremblings, and faint Sweats; I did not run
To Snatch the Laurel; and usurpe the wreath
To my owne Browes; but dasht with everie Breath
Of a supposed Censure, happilye lost
The Glorie of my Youth; then be it most   10
Abhorring to my Thoughts, to lay a new
Foundation; or varie from the true
Undoubted Rites of Poesie; or bring
But Cleare, and pregnant Reasons, any Thing.
This Ingenuitie, and Candor must
Allow of Force; and if a Schisme thrust
In all my verse, a monstrous Horne, or foot,
Cloven, to light of Judgment, blot me out
Of fair opinion; and my Name Ile give
Up, witts Apostate evermore to live.   20
     Nor would I yet be bitter; or engage
My selfe in Controversie, to the Age
With Sword and Buckler Language; but with all
The Modestie of Truth and Reason, call
A long spread error backe; and ratifie
Some proofes, to free me from this Heresie.
     Shall wee, who are made Judges then, and keepe
Minervaes holie Balance fall asleepe?
And let the giddie Rout give weight, and poise,
To Indesert? For Shame; Let us arise   30
And yet informe the Age. Shall wee derive

Our English Flame, our Glories Primitive
From antique Chaucer? blesse me witt; if right
Were onlie right, I feare, a present night
Would cover all his Credit. This I wage
Onlye for Truth; in reverence to the Age
Wherein he writt; but to the proof; and see
Her firme Records, kept by Mnemosyne.
  See, antique Greece; and see her in her Spring
Verdant and glorious; not lesse flourishing   40
At her first rise, then after; heare the String
Of sacred Orpheus, or hear Linus Sing;
Or to the Prince of All, Mæonides,
Attend with reverence; tell me; were not these
(When Learning hardly Crept) bright Suns? and Shine
Even to these Times of ours, with Light Devine?
Full in exalted Rapture, Poesie
Appeares in them, almost a Prodigie.
  Survay the Catalogue, of Splendent Rome:
Cæsar-supported Maro; yet by whom   50
Has he bene Equall'd, for a Steddie verse?
Wonder at Ovid, when Hee doth reherse
The Change of Things; what mightie flame doth fill
His varied Fancie, to enrich his Quill.
  A Thousand moe, in her bright Roll appeared
Of everie Nation, Poets, who, have rear'd
The Laurel famous; whom wee justlie Call
The learned Fathers of Apolloes Hall.
  And shall the seelie Age (with noise, and Stuffe
Like his owne writings) blow at Chaucers Snuffe? 60
To light our English Flame? where doth he rouse
The fresh pruned Feathers, of an Active muse?
Where doth he stretch a wing? or kicke his Clod?
But still his Fancie, is his greatest Load;
How liveles his Conceipts? he doth not rise
Like ancient Poets, in huge Extasies
Of uncontrolled Fancie, to Survay

45 (When Learning ... Crept)]; When (Learning ... Crept) Ms.

Inestimable nature; I might say
Much more, to vindicate this Argument,
That in-authenticke Chaucers furnishment,   70
Adds nothing to our Poesie, in his Store;
Nor let us call him Father, anie more.
    And you (who hardly out of Judgment) would
Seeme to defend him; cause you have bene told
Your Grandsires Laugh'd once at his Baud'rie
Laid out in Rime; (forsooth rare Poetrie!)
But where he comes the nearest, what you meane:
You'r wearie there your selv's, and leave him Cleane.
Perhaps you'le say, (as you have heard some say)
He was a glorious Poet, at that Day;   80
And why that Day? was Fancie in a Cage?
Rapture impounded? twas in the Darke Age
(As you would call it) when the former Sung;
Scarce then had witt, more then her mother tongue;
And yet they gain'd the Sphere, from whence wee bring
Our Cheifest Flowers, our best Embellishing.
    Forget Third Edwards raigne. They did not write
In that Age with the Spirrit they could fight;
For then Ide yeild (and in my Conscience wee
Use Pens, as well as Swords). Suffice it; Hee   90
Was disadvantaged of naught in Time,
But Language; which wee never made a Crime.
Why may not wee, better exempt his name
Then use it? adding nothing to our Fame;
And take the Radix, of our Poesie
To honour more, in this last Centurie;
The noble Sidney; Spencer liveing Still
In an abundant fancie; Jonsons Quill
Ever admir'd. These justly wee may call
Fathers; high placed, in Apolloes Hall;   100
But then wee want Antiquitie; as well
Dan Geoffrie wants his Age; for wee might tell
Of antique Brittish Druid's, and bring in

90   as well]; as wells Ms.

A hundred Rhiming Fellowes, that have bin
Tall Men at Meeter. One there was that Sung
I know not in what number, nor what tongue;
A gallant Storie, of Giganticke Feats,
Inchanted Castles, onsetts, and retreats
Innumerable; of a flying Bull
And six blue dragons. Oh most worshipfull,   110
Bring in these Fopperies; because they smell
Mustie, and antiquated; therfore well.
      Come to a Clearer Light; doe not delude
Your selves (heroicke English) to intrude
His name, the Cheif, in your faire pedigree.
Worthe is still worthy, in it selfe; were Hee
(Good Man) alive to heare it, sure as ought
Hee'd thinke, you lost more then hee ever taught;
To heare the Crue come in with open Mouth
And Crye, Oh Chaucer; Chaucer has a Tooth,   120
Oh perilous; and soe he had a Tongue;
Read him againe, heele shew you how it hung.
      But let not me, my first Designe outgoe;
(Which was upon Sound Arguments) to shew
A Spring more worthy, whence wee may derive
With greater Honour, the Prerogative
Of English Poesie; and clearlie evince
Noe Age can be call'd Darke, to a Cleare Sence;
As in the Ancients; this I doe, and must
Freely averre; which, if the Age will thrust   130
Upon me as an Heresie, how Cleare
Stand I to Judgment? I can never feare
Such Censure from the wise; and I contemne
Loud Follie, in a Thousand; fitteth them,
And Mee with them, better to let it fall
And please them, in a Canterburye Tale.

PREVENTION

Twas Late, and Cold; when with a mightie Flame
Possest, I, to my quiet Studie came,
Rich, in a high pitch'd Rapture; well compos'd
In everie Facultie; my thoughts dispos'd
In sober Contemplation, of a Brave
Designe in witt, a Fancie which might save
A Name to Honour; and almost create
Eternitie, and Time anticipate;
Quicke formed in each part; soe strong, soe pure
I could not wish a better; and Ime sure   10
The pregnant Age, a richer could not boast;
Which surelie might, (had Poesie bene lost)
Have rais'd a liveing flame. But (Oh the Sad
Curse of Posteritie) when now I had
Survaied it true, in all Dimension
Of perfect feature; and the holie Crowne
Had kist with humble Reverence; which then
I thought unrivalld Mine; and kist agen;
I had the rich Idea, in my braine
Soe livelie fitt, soe prest to entertaine   20
My willing Quill; and had my Pen soe neare,
I thought it done; but was prevented here;
The harvest of my Time, in which I thought
To reare my liveing Name, now fell to nought.
For busie, how to thawe my Jet to Inke,
It fled my Thought, before I ought could thinke;
That Peice, for which I thought from future Times
T' have gained whole Hecatombes, of Tribute Rhimes,
Lost in a Cloud, I know not how, nor where;
Nor doth a Member of that forme appeare.   30
Starrs inauspicious, never knew to Crosse
Our prosperous Muses, with a greater Losse;
When manie years hence, I this verse shall read,

'Twill Splitt my soule, with greife; when I am dead,
Deprived Posteritie, shall teare this Sheet,
Distracted in the Fate, to thinke how great
A flame might once have warm'd em. I could teare
A Rheme to Atomes; and all Quills forsweare
While I repeat it; had the greedie Flame
Snatcht all my Trifles, and but left my Name,   40
This Trophie; I had stood above all rage
Of Present Malice, or an ignorant Age;
This glorious fruite! halfe ripened! to be lost
In the Cold bowells, of a greedie Frost
Has raised in me a fire of Rage, to thawe
The Articke Circle, and make void all Lawe
Of winter, to the Russian. I could melt
Those ever Rocks of Ice, which never felt
One ray to warme them; make a Sea to Flow
Within the Continent, of Alpine Snow;   50
But I am blind in Furie; and transgress
All modest rules; loosing in Emptiness
Of Passion, future Glories; and almost
In Error, has my fantasie more lost
Then late, in Accident. Yet will I Charme
Thy Subtle power, fearing a future harme.
Let Winter dwell, upon the Island Shore
And with his breath, bind Shallow waters ore;
Fetter, in Guiues of Christall, the full Streams
Of Tanais, or Volgha; whilst our Thames   60
Runs with untroubled waters, in a Cleare
And even Course; thou hast noe Title here.
Why on my Standish, Tirant, didst thou fall?
Thou hast not right, to freeze an Urinall:
Doth not the bright-haird God, in glorie Shine,
(Throughout this Ile? to crush all Power of thine?)
Phebus assistant to all brave designe!
Ah then, why did he suffer this of mine
To perish? sure Hee is not as of old

(When witt Succeeded) antique Poets told 70
Soe much a freind, unto the harmonie
Of numbers, and true ayme of Poesie;
Either he never was, or he has lost
Latelie, the Soveraigntie, which they All boast;
Or if he be the Nourisher, of witt,
Why would he suffer Ice, to smother it?
Noe; Phebus is my foe; or he has Swore,
Since Jonson Dyed, t' allow his Heirs noe more.
I know not what to Judge; but if I live
Ile trye, this Fancie Fled, how to revive. 80

A STRANGE MAYE

THE EARTH, in her best verdure; and the Spring
As glorious as antique Fame, did Sing,
Her constant Tempe; all the Meads were sett
With bright Enamel; and the feilds were fitt
All most for the keene Sickle, which might seeme
Justly a wonder; if wee doe esteeme
Our colder Latitude; for who shall Say
(Without reproofe) the Harvest is in Maye?
Now Maye it was; what vast Hyperbole
Will serve but to speake truth? the blooming Tree   10
Crack't with its weight of Fruite; and wee almost
Might, by the Season, August have suppos'd:
All Eares were fill'd, and everie tongue could prate
Of Prodigie; and guesse, I know not what;
Some wiser, left it in the Misterie,
And from the Cause, look'd what th' effects might be;
The avaritious Husband, claw'd his Eare,
And deem'd to have, two Harvests in a Yeare.
Thus, stood the Earth; to Miracle almost;
When the more Miracle, a biteing frost   20
With a bleake northerne wind, orerun the feild
And nipt the Swelling Graine, the fruits it kill'd;
The painted Meadowes, chilled in their pride,
Grow wan; and flowers run backe agen, to hide
Themselves, in warmer Crannies of the Earth.
Never was such a Change since the great Birth
Which Chaos teemed; and though it Ruine threat,
Who knowes? but when the Sun, in better Heat
Shall mount his Throne in Cancer; with his rayes
May quicken them, and give a new encrease;   30
Soe satisfye our Hopes; that men may Say,
The Sun, in June, Conquer'd the Storme in May.

3   sett] Grosart. The Ms. is illegible; apparently the word *sett* has been
    written over the original, which may have been *settst*.

FREEDOME

I BLESSE my Starrs, I am unfitt for noise;
And busines all most shuns me, to my Choice;
I sitt retir'd, while other men are high
In State Employments; tis a peircing Eye
Sees thorough Men, to dispositions,
And sorts fitt Agents, to Occasions;
This with its Spectacles, Authoritie
Can Cull em by the head; and why should I
Repine? I glorie rather; and can Sitt
T' emprove by them, what may be Just, or fitt.   10
Ime happie, Ime exempt; that I may play
With my owne thoughts, unvext, my howers away;
I am not in Commission, of the Peace;
Noe Constable, the greater, nor the Lesse;
Ide nothing Glorie, if I had ben made
Poll' gatherer of the Groats; I should evade
Truly, to be a Parish warden; or
A domineering Elder; with the power
Our well-affected Parliament can give.
Fitt Men shall have Emploiment fitt; I live   20
Obscure; Blood, Tears, nor oppression
Burden my Soule: my Guilt is but my owne:
Whilest higher Sin, attends the higher place,
Sin of Participation in the Case.
I'me as I am, Content; and free, to pittie
The faction of the Countrie, Fraud o' the Cittie.
Sometime Ile take my Stone-bow, or my Gun
With my true Servant, readie still to run,
And fetch the Quarrie, from the Brooke or Bush,
The Mallard, Teale, the Sparrow, or the Thrush;   30
With these innocuous pleasures I can rest
In my selfe quiet; (and display the brest
Of all my Crime, unto my selfe) wee live
Guiltye, I hope of lesser Sins. I strive

Not now t'exaggerate others Crimes, nor here
To make our owne lesse then in Truth they are.
This, if the rigour of the times allow,
I am content; if they will not, I know
A pleasure 'bove their Malice; and the close
Barr's of a prison, cannot hinder those,   40
My owne free thoughts; where I sometime may have
A visit from the Muses, which shall save
My Name from Envie, and oblivion.
Soe being lest my selfe, I'me most my owne;
And what, by them, was put as a restraint,
Is by my patience, turned t' a Complement.

PROPORTION

MAN, (Screen'd, by Flesh and Blood, and wrapt within
Th' impenetrable Curtaine, of his Skin)
How shall wee pourtray out? what antique Quill,
Or famous moderne, boasts of such a Skill?
Not great Apelles, nor fam'd Titian
Had anie Colour, for the inward Man;
Much Celebrated Angelo, could give
Life to his worke almost, in perspective;
And our late honoured Vandike, may raise
Himselfe a Trophie, from anothers Face.   10
But this exceeds their Cunning; all wee know
Of this rests in our Selves, & what wee owe
Unto Philosophie; whose gentle hand
Can put aside the Vaile; and then wee stand
                    Naked, and plaine;
As in the outward face, and all the parts
Exterior; each severall imparts
A diverse Feature; & noe two can bee
Soe like in Face, such Twinn's in Symmetrie,
But a discerning Eye, may eas'ly find   20

A difference. Soe is it in the Mind:
Noe two in the same mold; and unto Each
(As in the Bodie Naturall) his pitch
Is limited; and not one Inch can adde
In Stature, to the measure that he had;
Nor Change his Face, to a Complexion
Fairer, then that which Nature made his owne.
Soe is the diverse Face of Reason; and
The understanding, cannot put a hand,
                    Beyond that Reine.   30
It now appeares, as plainly to my Eye,
The Mind, and Intellectuall Phisniomie,
As the Corporeall Shape; and I perceive
The same Discordances, which wee conceive
In all exterior formes; and Each man best
Suits with his proper owne. Can I divest
My Swartie Hewe? and put upon my face
A better Tincture? or new features place
Where the old were imperfect? Neither may
I put away my Reason; though it Stray   40
And be a Monster, to anothers Eyes!
Yet knitt soe Close unto my Faculties
It cannot part; noe more, then heat from fire,
A Qualitie Inhærent, and Entire.
                    It is the Same
In understanding; given severallie
To the proportion; & shall therefore I
Despise my selfe? because my Stature is
Perhaps an Inch, or Cubit, below his?
Because he (with a longer Arme) can reach   50
That thing with Ease, which I with all my Stretch
Cannot attaine? There is a height beyond
His utmost; Man is all of Pigmey kind;
And though our Giant understandings reare
Themselves, on Tiptoes, to the wished Sphere,
How are they lesse, then nothing? & his leape
Is but to fall againe; whilst others reape

A larger Harvest, with a lesser Toyle;
But noe man has the Stocke; noe Inke, nor oyle,
       Can bring a Name,   60
Beyond his Circumscribed Power. Wee All
Have proper Motions; and they rise, to fall
Unpittied, who adventure on a path
Of soe much ruine, as noe lesse then Death
Attends each Step; yet man, in Time, be wise.
Bee thy owne Mirror; See Deformities
As well as Beauties; and correct them there
With as much Diligence, and as great Care
As in a glass thy face, shouldst thou perceive
A Spott to lessen Beautie. Tis, beleive,   70
More worth thy Care, to rectifye this part
Then all thy Face. Bee happie, as thou art;
That is; Bee pleased with thy owne; and See
Some Creatures Creepe, as well as others Flee.

THE USERPER

I SAW THE WORLD; and wondred at the Sight;
(For I was raised above the common Light
Into that Region, where wee eas'lye see
All formes at once, mixed or diverslie)
Hence I look'd downe; and saw the Creatures, All
Fixt in theire Causes; and made Severall
To their distinct, and single Motion,
Which wee distinguish strangely, to our owne
Capacities; and Rationall prefer
Proper, alone to Man; the Beasts (more nere   10
Then Plants, or Trees,) wee call but Sensitive;
And those, by vegetation, meerly live.
     Or wee are blinded; or wee quite mistake
The Square, which wee our selves, our guide would make;

   5 Creatures,]; Creature, Ms.

If it be rationall to move, and live
A part, t' assist the whole; and each part give
His proper furtherance; and who most faile
To advance it, are most irrationall.
Man Cannot boast of Reason; (nor dispose
Defects, or Eminencies, unto those   20
Inferior Creatures), (Lordinge ore the rest)
Forfeit to his prerogative; the least
And most unprofitable member, in
His motion. Oh! how often have I bene
Dasht to the pit of Shame? to thinke man, made
His great Creators Image; and arrayed
With Glorie, next to Angells; and beyond
All other Creatures, both in Face and Mind;
Had Reason then; or what wee would define
By severall notions, to that gen'rall Line: 30
Made Lord of all the world, to use, and know:
A Thing soe sordid, and ignoble now
Wee cannot speake him; and the Creatur's vye
Forces, and foyle him; they imperfectlye
Move to their End; Hee, from perfection,
To this low step, is fall'n. Oh! haples Son
Of humane frailtye, yet in Time recall
Thy Birthright noble in th' originall;
And tis not lost to thee; leave of to speake
His Ruine; and his Reparation make.   40

THE MAGAZINE

RISE WITH THE MORNE, and gather up the Deaw;
              Flye to the East
And rifle all the Sweets, the Phœnix drew
              Into her Nest;
              Plunder the west,
Natures Exchequer; Search the Subtle wombe
Of waters, for their Wealth, and bring em home.

These are not of Content; but of Desire;
             Wee are our owne
Treasure, and wonder; if wee but Admire   10
             What wee have not knowne;
             These over-blowne
Will wast to nothing; but the living Store
Rests in our Selves, not seeking any more.

A PAUSE

G : IVE ME a little respite; that I may
        D : rawe somewhat of a better forme; to pore
E : ver on Bookes, takes all the Joy away;
        A : nd makes a freeborne Muse, her selfe abhorre.
O : h never may the Muses know, a Day
        N : ot given to Libertie; I will noe more
R : ifle my braines, to please Men; or to pay
        I : ust obligation; from thy liveing Store
G : rant me fresh raptures, Phebus, I will play
        E : asie, and quicke; but now I can noe more.   10
E : nvite me not (Deare Muses) to trye that
        L : ittle I have, against my owne Conceit.

THE END OF THESE FIRST POEMS

10 but now]; but not Ms.

Love Platonicke

A Small Poeme

FIRST WRITTEN 1642: BY
THE SAME AUTHOR;
TAKEN FROM THE ORIGINALL
INTO THIS PLACE COPIED;
1·6·4·6·

Non est forma Satis, nec, quæ vult' bella videri;
    Debet vulgari more placere Sibi;
Dicta, Sales, lusus, sermonis gratia, risus,
    Vincunt Naturæ candidioris opus;
Condit enim formam, quicquid consumitur artis,
    Et nisi velle subest, gratia tota perit.

TO CINTHIA; COYING IT

NOE LONGER Cinthia; have I spent
My time, but for a Complement?
            Have I read all
The Solemne Dictates, of a noble Love!
Taught all the Misterie, which doth behove
            A naturall
      Pure Flame to exercise?
      And you in Heresies
      Yet wander! noe more vexe
Your Selfe, in the Stale Error of your Sex.   10

Not any doctrine, in our Schoole,
    Tends, to the ruine of a Soule;
            You may be bold
To follow all our Precepts, and observe
A Stricter Modestie, then those who sterve
            Love, in the old
      Mantles of mother witt;
      They doe not know, the fitt
      Freedome of Nature, in
That Passion of the Soule, without a Sin.   20

Come; let me gather a new Flame
    From thy bright Eyes; the old is lame;
            And I forget
The better Principles, while I dispute
You into Faith. Come, tis a modest Suite,
            And might be writt,
      A vestal Canon. Fye,
      Tis meere Simplicitie
      To hinder your owne blisse.
Would you Assent, there were noe joy, to this.   30

The bruitish Passions of Lust,
Wee doe not know; nor the unjust
            Power of the will.
Our blood is Calme, and Cold; and all the root
Of Nature is Corrected; here noe doubt
            Can move that Ill,
      Your Ignorance suggests;
      Wee have more open brests
      And thinke, but what wee say;
And doe the Same, in the same free cleare way   40

      May I not yet enjoy the free
      Possession of my Selfe, in Thee?
            Let Men Suspect,
By their owne guilt, our Sin; it shall not move
Our Innocence. Daigne yet an Equall Love;
            Prize noe respect,
      To that Beatitude,
      Wise mortalls have pursu'd,
      With Free, and Chast desires;
Warmed with the best (now called) Platonicke fires.   50

TO CINTHIA CONVERTED

Come my Cinthia; gladly fixe
Thy bright, and Chaster Eyes, on mine;
Yet be free; and let us mixe
In noe base Corporeal twine;
But in the freedome, of our Soules embrace,
Knitt by the mutuall Glance, of Eithers Face.

Happie are the Minutes, which
Wee Spend and keepe, in this enjoying;
Tainted with noe Sordid Itch
Of sensuall Pleasures, ever Cloying.   10
Wee freely move, within our Selves; and Eyther
Moves in the other, one and both together.

My better selfe, in all the tye
Of Chast Affection, thinke I prise
Noe Joy, to this Societie.
Not all the Treasure of thy Eyes
Was such a forcive Character, to bind
My Love, as this great Sympathie of Mind.

Nor let the vulgar blame us in
Their owne surmises, fond and weake;   20
Wee are not guiltye of that Sin,
Which they are bold to doe, and Speake;
Let them Enjoy their Active heat; whilest wee
With Soules Combined, in our Selves are Free.

Dear Cinthia; breath thy Innocence
Into the Closet of my heart;
Whilst in a mixt Intelligence,
Wee Joyne the Soule, in every part;
Soe generate new Loves; and keepe entire
The Faculties, unstained with Desire.   30

CINTHIA CONFIRMED

CAN IT BE LOVE? which the rude Action
Of nature, may Compleat?
Or can the Sences Satisfaction
Proceed, from noble heat?
Can Love at once
Create, and Ruine? or an Ayme intend
To an ignoble End?
And yet advance
A Face of vertue? Love can never bend
Two wayes, at once.

TO THE PLATONICKE PRETENDER

DULL FOOLE; to mocke a flame
Beyond thy Fate;
Thou canst but prate
Of Common Love, veil'd in another Name;
The word Platonicke, pleases thy Conceit;
And some new thing
Thou wouldst have others understand, in it;
But canst not bring
One Accent, to evince
It from the Common Sins   10
Of Appetite, and naturall Desire;
The word, is all thy Flame.
Dull Sinner! doe not blame
These Just reproaches; if a Zealous fire
Let the world see,
A strange Hypocrisie.
For in Platonicke Love thou canst doe more
With yeilding Females, then in Lust before.

Ladies beware; he will deceive you, in
That Face of vertue, to the Act of Sin.   20

PURE PLATONICKE

Nᴏᴛ Rᴏsᴇs, joyn'd with Lillies, make
Her Faire, nor though her Eyes be blacke
And glorious, as th' Etheriall Queene,
Are they my wonder; I have seene
Beautie, and scorn'd it, at fowerteene.

Not to have a Skin, as smooth
As Christall; nor a Lip, nor mouth,
Bright Citherea's ornament,
Move me at all; let them invent
A Dresse, to move new blandishment,   10

I am not taken; not the Faire
Enchantments, of well-order'd haire,
Not a Leg, nor Foot, nor hand,
Nor the parts wee understand
Most attractive, mee command.

Though I give all Beautie prise
To the value of my Eyes;
Yet I doe not love a Face,
Nor dote upon the outward grace;
These respects, can have noe place.   20

Wee distinguish nothing to
The outward Forme, as Lovers doe;
Nor value by the rule, of Sence.
Wee know noe Sexes difference,
Equall in Pre'eminence

To the Sympathising mind,
Neither hinder, neither bind;
But in eithers brest wee move,
And Affections Equall prove:
This is pure Platonicke Love.   30

COURT-PLATONICKE

OH; BE FREE, as Equall ayre;
Though not soe gen'rall (my Faire).
Beautie doth attract the Eye,
In rayes, of the best Sympathye;
Here, I live Eternallye.

The darkest Day were richly Spred
In the full Treasure of your head;
The Earth unverdant may goe seeke
Her Flowers, in winter; but your Cheeke
Has all; and more, then wee can Speake.   10

Sabæan Gummes flye in your Breath
To recall Life, and ruine Death:
See it in me; for I noe more
Am liveing Man, then in the power
Of what your Kisses doe Secure.

The Tirant layes his Scepter by,
Commanded, by your awfull Eye,
And dares not Strike; if you but will
To have me Live. Oh; yet a while
Secure your Servant in your Smile.   20

Something moves within my Brest;
Something, not to be exprest;
Nature wills, when two agree,
Some nearer joyned Societye,
Then a discoursive Harmonye.

Let us perfect, all our worke;
Nature fires, should never lurke;
And the Act, alone can Seale
Mutuall Joyes; which to reveale
Were Treason; and I will not tell.   30

ANTI-PLATONICKE

Noe longer torture mee, in dreams
Of reservations, and Extream's;
Nature, never yet, in Two
Such a Calmenes, did bestow,
As you would pretend unto.

Give me buxome Youth; and Blood,
Quickned, in the understood
Caution of Love; a free desire
To meet with mine, in Equall Fire,
And doe the Act, wee both Conspire.   10

In the free, and Common way,
I would all my heats allay.
I have little Skill in love;
Little leasure, to Emprove
But by Natures precepts move.

In everie Step, I tread that path,
And to new Dictates, want a Faith;
If I see her yonge, and Faire,
Fresh, and Blith, and fitt to payre;
I have whol'some wishes nere.   20

My blood burnes; I cannot hold;
Strong desires make us bold;
I must utter all I thinke,
Not in a Question, or a winke:
Such mustie follies, ever stinke.

But I urge, and presse it close;
All I know, or you suppose;
Women are noe longer Chast
Then untempted; they would tast
Men, with Equall Heat, and Hast.   30

TO THE SWEET FEMININE
PLATONICKS

LADIES; (for only to the Feminine
Wee breath these gentle Ayres) it resteth in
Your power to raise us, (beyond all the right
Wee claime, to Poet) in this present Flight:
For love Platonicke, is a Dreame; (a Dull
Imperfect glance, of the most beautifull
Object our Nature claim's to) wanting you,
Who make that up an Act, was but a Show.

THE END

To THE READER, OF DOCTOR BROWN'S BOOKE
ENTITULED
PSEUDODOXIA EPIDEMIKA

IF TO DELIGHT, and profit, be of praise;
Admire this Author; who hath manie waies,
Oblig'd the world, in Eyther. Would yow see
Error unveil'd, by a Strict Scrutinie?
Would you know probablye, the Causes hid
Of many Things, in Nature? such as (bred
Upon the Pillowe of conjecture) were
Strangelie imposed, by Inquisition, Cleare?
Read ore this Booke. Or would yow trifle out
Your Time, in some unnecessarie Doubt?   ·   10
Seeme wittye? to discourse, of things unknowne,
As in your Knowledge? make this Booke your owne.
If a neat Stile, or Language, doe delight yee,
Fall gladlie to; nor let the Hard words fright yee.
Or, are yow Serious? would yow faine behold
Man, first Deluded? and the manifold
Still-interposeing Clouds, blearing his Sight
To looke at Truth, in her Eternall Light?
This, be the Mirror. I have said Enough,
As my owne Relish to it, drawes Mee through;   20
What yet remains is All; but What is That?
Reade ore the Booke, and Yow may tell Mee, What.

                                        G: Daniel.
Decembr: 11:th:
　1·6·4·8·

Upon an Excellent Treatise
WRITTEN BY T:B:D:M:
CALLED:
RELIGIO MEDICI

I HAVE NOT SEEN, (let me speake modestlie)
A finer Peice, of Ingenuitie,
Then in these Leaves laide out. When I survay
This Bodie, I am rapt; and loose my way
With wonder, and Delight; soe caught, soe tyed
I have noe Power to Change, to looke aside.
For who can fixe, upon a vulgar Face?
To such a beautie? whose abundant Grace
Strikes each Beholder; in such Similies
Wee humor Sence; and raise but Fantasies.   10
     I now, decline em here; and would not fill
This Page with varnish, of a trifling Quill;
But give a cleare round Sence; for 'twer in Mee
An Error sure (almost Impietie)
To be reserved; and that I may not blanch
My owne Conceptions (though with Ignorance
Perhaps Enough) take it in Short: I find
The livelie Image, of a freeborne mind
Speake, in a Stile soe Cleare, a Sence soe full,
I hardlie know an Equall; nothing Dull,   20
But with a Spirrit, the same still; though in All
I cannot joyne; but to the rationall
Exception, as each Genius intends
A severall way, and unto severall Ends;
Let me but varie, to my owne, as hee
To his owne Reason bends, (and certainlie
Hee limitts noe man) and I cannot fall
For Distances in Some, to leave in All
This Authour; whom I honour much, and prise
His generous Attempt; who would make wise   30
Deluded Men, and from Infirmitie
Erect a Structure of Abilitie.

Who sees his wants, is wise. Hee more, who can
Supplye his owne; and bring a Stocke to man;
Man-generall, from whence in full repaires
A Strong-built Edifice, Each man appears.
  These are the Fruits, of his industrious Pen;
T' unvaile himselfe, and informe other men;
Soe naturallie plaine, soe simply cleare,
I know him by his Booke, as were Hee here;   40
For it must bee Himselfe; and tis Enough
Reading this Booke, the man himselfe, to know;
To which great Character, what man dares thinke
(Fondlie Audacious) to adde with Inke?
Hee is above the vanitie, of Praise;
And what wee add's, below him manie waies.
  I know he has a mind, soe free, soe full,
Hee onlie writes Himselfe, and would not pull
Any, of Force, to follow in the Tracke
Hee paceth out; nor keeps Hee any backe;   50
But Each may move within his proper Sphere
And bee with Him, as free, as Hee is here
With all the world. Then with enlarged minds
Receive a worthie Guest; but my Sence binds
Onlie my Selfe; and I should prejudice
You; (Equall Readers) all Capacities
May (to their Strengths) Judge others witt; and none
Is limited, by my opinion;
Or by the Square I move by. I am free
To Truth, to Honour, and to Industrie;   60
And what I raise, is not to bring my owne
Name, as a Second, or Intruder, on
Fames Theatre, and more securelie sitt
Under the Penthouse of anothers witt.
  I have noe End, noe Ayme; beyond the free
Acknowledgment, how it hath taken Mee;

46 add's,]; add^e,s, Ms.; add^e, Grosart.
56 You; (Equall Readers)]; You; (Equall Readers;) Ms.; You, (Equall
    Readers); Grosart. The punctuation here chosen is consistent with
    Ms. practice.

And All I thinke on, is but what to Say
To such a Freind, as I can never pay.
It is beyond my Stocke, and all I can
Alledge Excuse, is: I'me but a poor Man.   70
It is Enough; I know, for that hee'le spare me;
I have it under's Hand within to cleare me.
Tis time I make an End: Each, as he list,
Pursue his Thoughts; and wander, in the mist
Of his Affections; I am pleased to looke
At men, in the cleare Mirror of this Booke.

August:1º Die:
    1 6 4 6

To my honored cozen t:cr:esqr: an affectionate invitation

If Flesh and Blood, or Prudee's name, could charme;
You might appear at Beswicke; but Ile arme
You, with more prejudice, then you suspect.
Our Feilds are barren; three daies, full erect,
(Pardon the word) in Expectation
T' have seene you here; the purest Distillation
Our villages are proud of, is broke through
The double Limbecke; and ther's none for you.
        Tom: if you Laugh, Ime angrie; to appease
That Furie, let me meet you, where you please.   10
I hope our Lockinton, may yet produce
Some thriftie Chimist's Store; something of Juice
Which (though not Spirritt) may a Spirrit raise;
You know in diverse men, how manie waies;
In mee, noe fire can mount, beyond that Sphere
I place my best freinds in; and you are there.

                    This hastilie, from Dear Cozen:
February:26:   G:D:
    1 6 4 6:

To THE MEMORIE OF THE EXCELLENT
DRAMATIQUE ENGLISH POETS:
MR FRA: BEAUMONT: & MR JO: FLETCHER
UPON THE IMPRESSION OF THEIR SEVERALL
COMEDIES TRAGEDIES, &c.

I KNEW YOU NOT; therefore what I may say
Is free from Passion; other People may
Distinguish in your workes; which unto mee
Appears like Sizors of Impietie,
To part the Webbe, which you still kept intire
And loved it Soe. As in the Globe, noe higher
Nor lower, properlie is understood;
Soe in your orbed witt, I know noe Flood
To drowne the others Earth; noe Element
But was soe pois'd, it made one Excellent,   10
Equallie moveing Sphere. Others, who knew
Your severall parts, may give, as they thinke due;
For me, I am forbid; what you thought fitt
To joyne (Your Selves) I will not Sever itt.
Fletcher, and Beaumont! who shall ere devide
These noble Twinn's? Twins, by the Surer side;
Crossing the vulgar mouth, who gape, and Yawne;
Credit, or Kindred, meerlye by the Spawne;
And can see nothing higher. Mother witt
Was still their Charter; & they claime by't yet.   20
You, Sons of Phebus, (bright as his owne Light
Unto our Ile, late wrapt up in the night
Of Ignorance, where witt might but appeare
Like owles, in Twilight) have redeem'd us here;
And like those happie Fires, (Auspicious still
To Navigators, joyn'd; if Single, ill
And Fate-portending) you revived have
Witts Barke, long tost upon a dangerous wave;
And Shine, to guide and Comfort those, who trye
That ocean, for some new Discoverie.   30
If there be any world, beyond what you

Have given Maps for; Straights which none yet know,
Yet some shall undertake; Your joyned Flames
Direct em; who, to Celebrate your Names,
Shall Pillars raise inscribed, by what Light
They past the false Fires: & arrived right
In the safe Port, of   — thus to you
Future Endeavours, must be ascribed too.

Soe long as Socke, or Buskin treads the Stage,
Beaumont and Fletcher shall enrich the Age;   40
Or Should the Malice, of hot mouth's proceed
To Silence Theaters; let even Witt bleed
To death in Catharr's, and the raging fire
Of Envie, Swallow truth, when they expire.

G: Daniel

An ode
UPON THE INCOMPARABLE LIRICKE POESIE
WRITTEN BY MR GEORGE HERBERT;
ENTITULED;
THE TEMPLE

Lord! yet how dull am I?
When I would flye!
Up to the Region, of thy Glories where
Onlie true formes appeare;
My long brail'd Pineons, (clumsye, and unapt)
I cannot Spread;
I am all dullnes; I was Shap't
Only to flutter, in the lower Shrubbs
Of Earth-borne-follies. Out alas!
When I would treade   10
A higher Step, ten thousand, thousand Rubbs
Prevent my Pace.

37 The lacuna occurs thus in the manuscript.

This Glorious Larke; with humble Honour, I
                    Admire and praise;
                    But when I raise
My Selfe, I fall asham'd, to see him flye:
The Royall Prophet, in his Extasie,
                    First trod this path;
Hee followes neare; (I will not Say, how nigh)
      In flight, as well as faith.   20
Let me asham'd creepe backe into my Shell;
      And humbly Listen to his Layes:
Tis prejudice, what I intended Praise;
As where they fall soe Lowe, all Words are Still.
      Our Untun'd Liricks, onlie fitt
            To Sing, our Selfe-borne-Cares,
      Dare not, of Him. Or had wee Witt,
            Where might wee find out Ears
Worthy his Character? if wee may bring
                  Our Accent to his Name?   30
This Stand, of Lirick's, Hee the utmost Fame
Has gain'd; and now they vaile, to heare Him Sing
Horace in voice; and Casimire in winge.

                              G: Daniel.
Decemb: 8t:
1.6.4.8:

   13 This Glorious Larke;] first Ms. version; happie Larke;   second Ms.
       version.
   33 Horace]; Horace? Ms.; Bocace Grosart. In his second version of the
       poem, Grosart prints the correct reading.

Scattered Fancies

FORMERLIE WRITTEN, IN SEVERALL
LOOSE PAPERS,
NOW DRAWNE UP IN A
LIRICKE POESIE;
1645

By the Same Author:

CARMEN PROTREPTICON
LECTORI:

Men looke on Poems; but they doe not reade
Them to the Sence, which makes the Fancie deade
And circumscribes the Author, in a fewe
Smooth running Words; but if you passe a Due
Censure on Writers, ayme at judging well;
Weigh everie word, and everie Sillable;
And though you read em twice, and something find
To strike your Fancie, thinke there is behind
Another Sence, worth all that you have knowne;
The Poet made em Such; and that's His owne.

TO THE READER:

I DARE NOT soe much Affront Poesie, as goe about to vindicate her with a Prose Apologie; or Soe much derogate, from that clear Source; as borrow water, from the muddled Cisternes of her Inferiour: but this, I not insist upon; neither need it Springe any Controversie. What I have now to say is but to the ingenious Reader, that Hee will value these, noe other then as the writer gives them Leaves, and perhaps Budds of a tree, which (if this long winter of generall Calamitie had not nipt, and nere perished) might have brought forth a more noble, and better relishing Fruit. These are but short-breathings of a Sad, (though I speake clearlie) not dejected Mind; nor can I (which to the common Reader will be blameable enough) give a Severall Title to these Trifles, changing occasion haveing the best Title to them All; soe that, in Some I have bene lost, and Swallowed from my first intentions, by newer thoughts, but of these not many: which will easilie present themselves to Him I direct this Poesie.

SCATTERED FANCIES

ODE I

When I am gone, and these of mine remaine,
If these, or ought which I call mine, shall Stay,
   Read over what I leave, and you againe
Adde to the Sand of Time; and give my Day
     As glorious Life, as when I stood to breath:
     Hee Dyes not; who Survives his Dust, in Death.

I doe not Beg a Life, beyond my Fate,
Or aske the Courtesie, you would not give;
   Tis neither You, nor I, can set a Date
To written Numbers, if a Muse bid live.
     And these may Live; who knowes, when winds disperse
     My Earth in Atomes, Men shall read this verse.

ODE II

1

How much a verse deceives,
Unhappie man! who weaves
   His hopes upon it?
Thinking to gaine a grace,
From some light wantons face,
   With lighter Sonnet;
His Thoughts, his Hope, his Fate hang all upon it.

2

To Titles, or great Name,
One brings an Epigram,
   Yet scarce knowes why;
Another, comes too late
Deploreing humane Fate

In Elegie:
Praising a name to Raise his owne more high.

3

Some, Souce in bitter Inke,
The venome, which they thinke,
    To taxe the Times:
Write Satire, to betray
Selfe-guilt, whilst they display
    The Ages Crimes,
And vindicate their owne with biting Rhimes.

4

Some in a higher Straine,
Must Annalize the Raigne
    Of Cæsars Glorie;
Breath big, and thunder State,
Lest he extenuate,
    And dimme, the Storie,
Which, his muse tells him, is not Transitorie.

5

Another, doth prefer
To the full Theater,
    His giddie verse;
Now, in a Comicke Stile
Hee wantons; in a while,
    Growne bit, and feirce,
The buskind Muse comes out, in Blood and Tears.

6

How much the verse deceives
Our hopes? like Autumne leaves
    They blow away;
The Time wee spent, is lost;
And onlie Time can boast,

In our Decay:
Our verse forgot, not one Line left to Say:

7

Great Monster, shall wee gaine
Our Labour for our paine?
And noe more wage?
Ile bring, to stop thy Jawes,
And Cancell all thy Lawes
Of Right, or Rage,
A Verse, too Stronge for Envie or for Age.

ODE III

1

Give me the Sober Muse, and Simple Thought,
To furnish out my Loome;
Let others come,
As they affect, in finer garments Clad:
Happilie farder fett, and dearer bought.
If I had sought such, Such I could have had
At the same rate;
But I decline that State:
Give me the Sober Muse, and Simple Thought.

2

Expect noe fine Thing here, noe gaudie knacke;
But Course and Common Things;
Our Larum rings,
Not to the giddie Eare, who seekes the Chime,
Of Scurril Language; or affects the Smacke
Of Brothel-feats laid Centinel in Rime,
How to betray
Soules to a Sad Decay:
Expect noe fine Thing here, noe gaudie knacke.

3

Oft have I bene deceived; but ofter you,
　　　　Whose Joy in fired blood
　　　　　　You make your good;
　　And pant, to see a Fancie Set to light
　That may blow up old fire; or adde a new
　　　Unmanlie itching, to the feeble Spright.
　　　　　　Let your thoughts move
　　　　To somewhat, worthie of your Love:
Oft have I bene deceived, but ofter you.

4

Repent it, ere too late; Repent in Time
　　　　　　The Error of your witt;
　　　　　　　Thinke it unfitt
　　For high-borne man, soe poorlie to decline;
　Scorne sordid Earth; and Joy in the Sublime
　　　Raptures of Truth, clad in the liveing Shine
　　　　　　　Of modest Fire;
　　　　　And hate your old Desire:
Repent it ere too late; Repent in time.

5

Goe, learne the better Arts of Innocence;
　　　　　Which will instruct you, how
　　　　　　To scorne what now
　　You sought with Eagernes; and to your Soule
　Propose a richer prize, at lesse expence;
　　　Where the true pleasure lives, without controule
　　　　　　　Of Doubt, or Feare;
　　　　　One other Step will bring you there:
Goe, learne the better Arts of Innocence.

6

Error has many waies, t'entrap a Soule;
　　　　　　A thousand more
　　　　　　　Then wee Account her Store;

Changing to everie Sence, with what they please,
Now Light, now fixed; Sometime seeming foule
Unto the Sence; when She the Sence doth seize
With greater might,
And with as great Delight:
Error has many waies, t'entrap a Soule.

7

Depart, false seeming Joyes; fond mirth Depart;
Treachers of old;
Growne in our Age, more bold;
Light, hopes, and feirce Affections quit the place;
Lay by your Tirant Scepter; for my heart
Is free to Truth, disdaining Servile waies
Of blinded Sence,
And Passions large pretence:
Depart, false seeming Joyes; fond mirth depart.

8

Am I not Sworne a Denizon to Truth?
A free Associate,
Within that State,
Where heaven-bred Peace is Queene? Onlie to her
I vow the remnant of my halfe-spent youth;
And never lend false Smiles, an Eye, nor Eare;
Noe more Suggest
Your pleasures, to my brest:
Am I not Sworne a Denizon to Truth?

9

Nere may my Thoughts Swerve, from their fixed home;
But here in Raptures dwell;
Which none can tell
Who, blind with Error, run in Sensuall waies;
And though the blood-fired Ruffian, rageing come,
With Scorne against my verse; and Spend his praise
In Balladrie,

Defending Luxurie:
Nere may my thoughts swerve, from their fixed home.

10

Just now he frownes, to Strike the Poet dead,
If Eyes could wound, or kill;
And calls them Ill,
The verses he has read; and Sweats, and Swears
A brain-sicke Frensie overburdened,
Has run a Larum, to abuse his Eares;
And bring a Cold
Ere years, to make him old:
Just now he frownes, to Strike the Poet dead.

11

Erect that drowsie head, and yet see Day;
See; the bright Skies
Would Shoot into thy Eyes,
With Glorie, to informe misguided Sence;
Yet be a Man; and heare what all men Say:
There is a way of Truth, and Excellence,
Where Joy and love,
Will teach the Soule, to move:
Erect that drousie head, and yet see Day.

12

Let others Sing of Love, and loose delights;
My sober Quill, has vowed
(Though understood
Perhaps by few) to use her Inke, in praise
Of glorious vertue; this, the irkesome nights
Shall melt; and be the labour of my Dayes;
This Sacred Straine,
My howers, shall entertaine:
Let others Sing of Love, and loose Delights.

ODE IV

1

Our Muses, not exiled, with Sober Feet
Draw forth Sad numbers, to a heavie Straine;
        And entertaine
Some Sparke of hope, they may renew the heat
        Of Rapture yet;
Though frequent Sorrowes, from Just Causes spring;
Some little Ayre, raises my nummed wing;
        And Nature, not yet old in Years,
        Would Stop the torrent of my fears,
        To Strike the Liricke String.

2

The thicke Ayre hangs, in Fogs about my head;
And many Thoughts, make my Sad Heart as Dull;
        My brest is full
Of mists and Clouds; my Fancie cannot Spread,
        (Oreburdened).
Her features, to the Life, I did intend;
When I begin, it dyes, and makes an End;
        In broken grones, abruptly closing,
        A Thousand of her beauties loosing,
        Beauties, which none can lend.

3

Come; yet a little, let our Thoughts forgett
Theire torture; and some pettie Solace find.
        If a sad Mind
Can but a little calme her Sorrowes; let
        The Muses heat
Breath gentle Rapture, interposing Fears,
And Sing our deep Cares, unto patient Ears;
        Who wounded, will not scorne our End
        Well leveil'd, though (ill Shott) it bend
        In a Distracted verse.

ODE V

1

Where, where resides content?
    The joy, which mortalls faigne?
Tis neither, in Extent
    Of Power, nor full-mouth'd gaine;
Nor in the Emptie Shade
Of honour, nor in Trade;
Nor in vast riot, nor in Swelling boules;
    Nor what wee pleasure call
    Diversified. The wall
Of Pallaces are emptie as the holes
    Of Scorned Peasants. Wee may looke
    The universe, in everie nooke,
And Cherish giddie Fancie, that wee shall
    Find, what is not at all;

2

For wee may apprehend
    Full joy, in the pursuit
Of our desires, which End
    Before they come to fruit.
Soe doe I often borrow
My pleasures, from the morrow;
It comes; and yet my Joy has noe more Life.
    For what can Time produce
    But moveing? Never thus
Will I be Slave, to Transitorie Strife.
    I will propose, unto my Soule
    A Pleasure, beyond Times controule;
A Path, where Innocence shall teach my Muse
    The Raptures she would Chuse;

3

And there find out, what Mortalls, with their Sweat
    Could never gett;

And in the Sober heights of vertue, Clime
    To goodlie ravishment;
Untouch't by Envie, un-impaired by Time;
For to be free, with a heart Innocent,
    Is onlie true Content.

ODE VI

1

    Noe more;
   Let me a while be free,
To my deare Muses; exercise your power
    On other men, not me;
    I am a freeman; know
    I am my Selfe; and you
Can but pretend, (at best) for what you fight;
Long usurpation, cannot give you right.

2

    Tis mine;
  The heart, you would subdue,
And Challenge by prescription, in a twine
    Of many years, to you;
    I will in the high Court
    Of Justice, make report
Of my Sad Case; and beg, on bended knees,
I may have right, from him who all wrong Sees.

3

    Tis true;
  You entred, by a sleight,
Upon my simple nonage; for you drew
    A faire pretext of right;
    Few freinds (god wot) I had,
    To give advice, or ayde;
But I must yeild my Earlie years, to those
Who strangers were, and were indeed my foes.

4

          Now man;
       Shall I be Slaved Still?
And kept a Child with Trifles? Noe; I can
       Not soe forget the Skill
      By nature lent; my years
      Are now past Childish fears;
And my free Spirrit scornes, to obey your power:
Goe seeke an orphan; I am yours noe more.

ODE VII

  1

Loe where Hee comes; the Monarch of the Earth,
       In Royall Scarlet Clad;
       Such objects make me Sad;
Is this a Time for Glorie, or for Mirth?

  2

With azure wings, and golden Diadem,
       A thousand vassals waite
       Upon his goodlie State;
And giddilie, the Rout his Shadowes hemme.

  3

Who this Should be, the Judging Reader knowes;
       Ah, sadlie I dare say,
       Hee did attend this Day,
Upon the monster, if he bend his browes;

  4

For in the front, of his Retinue Stands
       Bold Ignorance, the first;
       And ostentation, nurst
By the same brest, and swathed in the same bands.

5

These, misinforme the gaping multitude;
> And Chatter out his Praise
> To them, a thousand waies;
What Scepters he has won, what Lands Subdued;

6

For doubtles, great Hee is; though greater farre
> Hee be in their report
> Who limitt out his Court,
To the wide Gire, of Heavens still moveing Carre.

7

Let not their golden Sonnets Credit gaine,
> In your Judicious Eyes;
> Hee has in shamefull wise
Bene baffled oft; and may be soe againe.

8

A Shepheards Boy, who heard him proudlie boast,
> Bearded the Monster late;
> And triumpht in his Fate;
Whose lookes erewhile, had Cowed a mightie Hoast.

9

Yet Still he lives; for he can never Dye,
> Till Time and motion Cease;
> Till then, he shall increase
In all the Glories, of his Tirrannie.

10

A thousand, thousand Times, Hee has bene foyled;
> And where he most doth raigne,
> Hee formerlie was slaine;
By weaker hands, of a small Infant Child.

11

This, this is hee, of whom old Poets sung,
      Who more then once, was slaine;
      And still revived againe;
Nor could Hee dye, upon his mother flung.

12

There is an Art taught, where true Arts are taught;
      (For tis not strength alone
      Prevailes against his bone)
Will foyle him soone, and bring his strength to naught.

13

Then be not danted, my amazed Soule;
      The Giant, (were Hee more
      Then his owne vants) were poore,
To Cope with Boyes, instructed in this Schoole.

14

Thither, will I betake me; and there trye
      What Sleights will most prevaile;
      To make his Footing faile;
Till I be perfect in the Misterye.

15

Then muster up Collossus, to affright
      Stupid, and retchles Men;
      Who know, nor how, nor when,
Nor why, they yeild; their exercise, thy might;

16

And I will Sing away my Common Cares,
      With everie Sand of Time;
      Where Rapture shall Sublime
My new-borne Soule, in an immortall verse.

ODE VIII

1

Oh, how I wander! Oh, where shall at last
My wearied feet have rest? my mind repast?
Where shall I find, the wished Port of rest,
To Strike away the Fears, which have opprest
        My wounded Brest?

2

Long Dayes, I travell; bitter nights, I wake;
Till Heart, and Head, with overwatching ake;
I count the Atomes, of Times running Glasse;
And thinke the Howers, (which once did fleetly passe)
        Slow as an Asse.

3

I wonder Time can be soe patient;
My bowells burne, till all his glasse be spent;
The night brings horror; day gives noe releife
To my Affliction; one continued greife
        Weares out my Life.

4

Some pious Hand, direct me; I have gone
From Pole to Pole; and left, where I begun.
I tooke the wings, which for the Day were drest;
Survaied the orient, to the utmost west,
        But found noe Rest.

5

Yet, yet at length, let my spent Bodie find
A short repose. Oh, would you be soe kind,
You, who can onlie perfect mans desire,
And give that Rest; to which I now Aspire;
        A Rest entire.

6

Then should my Soule, in mightie Raptures move:
Where Sacred Rapture, fires it all in Love;
And joyne my String, to that Celestiall Quire
Whose Harmonie, is one united Lire,
   Of Sacred Fire.

7

There Centred, Rest in all her Joyes doth Rest;
Full in her Peace, with Joy and Glorie Blest;
Still may wee travell out our Age, in Feare,
To find that upon Earth, which is noe where,
   But onlie there.

ODE IX

1

  Goe dote, fond Lover; Seeke
   (To smooth lascivious Rhime)
   Some beautie, where Sublime
  Graces adorne the Cheeke;
    Court Lips, or Eyes,
    Or what you prise
With most Affection, as you can devise.

2

  And see, how long they please
   The flitting Sence with Joy;
   Either they kill, or Cloy,
  And aggravate Disease;
    Noe reall good
    Is understood,
Where the maine object is, but Flesh and Blood.

3

  But, if you would behold
   A Beautie, to Entice;

Revert your pur-blind Eyes,
Too blind, and yet too bold;
Ile Shew you, here
In her true Sphere,
Perfection, crowned in a golden Chaire;

4

Gainst which, the Rage of Time,
Could never yet prevaile;
Nor doth She want the Haile,
Of Poets, in a Rhime;
Remaining yonge,
Although she sprunge,
Ere time the Chaos into Forme had flung.

5

Nor Shall you need, to bring
Attributes to her praise;
For her Aspect will raise
A Store, too vast to Singe;
Such as would pose
Art to disclose
In any verse; and fill a Rheme of Prose.

6

This is that Beautie, which
Strikes dead all humane Sence;
From whose sole Influence,
All Creatures are made rich,
And what wee praise
Soe manie waies
Are but light Sparkes, shot from these liveing raies.

7

Bring, bring the loftie verse;
And Sonnet out your Dayes;
Let everie word be praise;

And everie Accent peirce
The Ears of Men
With wonder; when
You faile, goe to this Source, and fill your Pen.

8

Here, never Ending Love
Runns in a liveing Streame;
Peace sitts under the Beame
Of Glorie; all that move
Is holie, here;
Pale Doubt, and Feare,
Exiled are, and Envie comes not neare.

9

The witts, who sung of old
Their feilds of lasting pleasure,
Meant this; though in some measure
(Perhaps) it would not hold;
For, humane witt
Can onlie Fitt
The Sence with Joy; Soe much they failed of it.

10

Bring in fresh Chaplets; Crowne
Her, worthy all your praise;
And mightie Rapture raise
To sing her Name; lay downe
Your brittle Theame,
Caught in a Dreame;
And raise a Character, in her great name.

ODE X

1

The Day was Darke; and Heaven, his bright face Shrouds,
     In Sable Clouds;
The gaudie Sun, in his Meridian Light,
     Was Darke, as Night;
   And horrid Stormes, came rolling on the Skye;
   The Thunder Strucke, the Lightning feirce did flye;
The Ayre incensed, all her Streames let fall;
   The Cataracts of Heaven, theire Doores set ope,
     Whose gushing Torrents call
   Fresh Floods, to crosse the avaritious Hope
Of Men; to looke it should be faire at all.

2

My Sober Muse can say how it did wound
     My Sinnew-bound
Unusefull Members; how my Sence was dull
     And my Soule full
   Of horror and amazement; I had lost
   The nearest faculties, that life could boast;
Strucke with the Feare, into an Extasie
   Of Feare, like Death; indeed halfe dead with Feare;
     Yet knew noe reason why.
   I summond all my Sences in, to beare;
But they were Dead, with my Soules Agonie;

3

When loe, a glance of heavens Immortall ray,
     Found out a way
(Through the vast mure of Night) into my Soule
     And did controule
   My Stupid Sences; putt away my Feare;
   Made stronge my frailtie; and my doubts made cleare
That recollecting all my Thoughts, made new,

And weighing the late cause, of this Affright,
    Untroubled Heavens I veiwe,
  The Sun unclouded, and the Welkin bright;
Onlie, the Storme was in my bosome true.

*

For unto him, that hath a troubled Spright;
Time has noe Joy, nor Heavens bright Face, noe Light.

ODE XI

1

And now, tis Faire; how shall wee Spend the Day?
    Manage the lustie Steed?
Or see the Eager Hounds, pursue the pray,
    And laugh to see him bleed;
How shall wee run the lingring howers away?

2

Goe see the Gallant Falcon, from her wings,
    The Quarrie Strike?
Or stay to heare Hermogenes who Sings
    Soe Angel-like?
Or see the Fouler, lay his treacherous Strings;

3

Or with the baited Hooke, in Deviaes Streame,
    Beguile the simple Trout?
Or rather take a Gun, and warre proclaime
    To all the Birds about?
Or Sitt, and talke, and make the Times our Theame?

4

And where wee faile, the pleasures of the House
    Shall our Discourse supplie.
Plumpe Bacchus makes the heart glad, when he flowes

In Cups not niggardlie.
Or shall wee wage, what wee fear not to loose?

5

Some toy at Dice? or Cards? or will you tosse
  A Ball, att Tenis? or
Lets boule an hower or two, with the same losse:
  Our Time, wee loose noe more;
Or Billiards, or what Else, you will propose.

6

Come, shall wee wanton with a Ladies Eye?
  And Appetite provoke?
Or keep the Round of good Societie
  In high-pris'd Indian Smoke?
And let the novice breake the Pipes, lye by?

7

Lets this, or any these, which you like best
  Pursue; the Day growes old;
The Sun is halfe his Journey to the west;
  But if to morrow hold,
With better pleasures wee will be refresht.

8

Were we but now made dull, with Stormie Ayre!
  And shall we use it thus?
That Day, which (Doubtles) heaven did prepare,
  To fitt us, in an use
More Noble; which wee loose, ere wee' are aware.

9

Come, take thy Quill along, my Sober Muse;
  And wee will find a place,
Where wee may freelie Sing, and shade our Browes
  Under some Mirtle base.
Such humble Shrubs, my Thoughts doe rather Chuse.

10

Or shall wee, under crooked Hawthrone Sitt,
    And our Sad Fancies dresse?
Or rather chuse our loved Elme? and fitt
    Notes, to our heavinesse?
Not Emulous of Fame, nor Glorious of witt?

11

However, where wee Sitt, or what wee Sing,
    The Day shall be made short,
In sober recreations; when the wing
    Of Fancie, flyes to sport,
Heaven, Ayre, Earth, Water, all their beauties **bring:**

12

And be the Day, or Clear, or cloudie Dull,
    Our pleasure is the Same:
To morrowes Expectation cannot gull
    Our Thoughts, in their true Ayme;
Nor take from what wee seeke, in objects full.

13

Thus then, he pleasure only doth enjoy,
    Whose pleasure is not tyed,
In change of time, to quicken, or destroy,
    But more securely ride
All winds and weathers, with a Constant Joye.

*

Him, nor the Angrie Heavens can Affright;
Nor Serene Skies please, with a better Light.

ODE XII

1

Contented I, to frame a rurall ode,
    In humble Shades;
Admire those Swains, who in bright Southerne Glades,
    Doe make abode;
And Carol high to Fame, with mounting Quill;
My obscure Groves, best suit my humble Skill.

2

Let me, unto the fameles Deviaes Shore,
    Low Accents frame,
Unenvied in my Fate, or in my Fame;
    And raise my Store
From noe mans Harvest, but a Stocke produce
From native bounties, to enrich my Muse;

3

And run, with changing Chords, as Fancie guides
    To everie new
Object of Chance; which wee will more pursue,
    The more it slides,
And gather a fresh Stocke, from all wee see,
Our numbers Charged, in varietie.

4

My Temples bound, not in a wreath of bay;
    (For be it farre
From my free Thought soe high Attempt to dare)
    But humble Hay,
May rest secure; and if I be content,
My Fate is better, Fame as Eminent.

5

There will I sing vast Nature, in her Store;
    And sing the Power

Which gives to Nature all her wealth; the bower
        Of All (and more)
Perfection; where all fullnes doth remaine,
Parent to Nature, who doth All sustaine.

6

Nature, made faire, in all her best Attire
        Brings it from hence;
Her weakest Ray, her beames of Excellence,
        Shoot, from one fire;
And not her lest production but doth Stand
A powerfull wittnes of his mightie Hand.

7

As Life, and Forme, did from his breath proceed;
        In the same way
Comes Sence-depriveing Death, and Sharpe Decay;
        Wee doe not tread,
But a fresh wonder rises, to display
Its beauties, Sparkes from the Eternall Ray.

8

A thousand Times, I contemplate his Store,
        In earthlie Things;
I yet rise higher, and my Judgment brings
        A Thousand more;
Yet treebled, and I looke upon the Sun
To gather new, and End where I begun.

9
There is noe Day soe Sad, noe night soe Dull,
        But I can meet
Ten miriads of wonder; and forget
        That I am full;
From nothing (be it scorned) but I can gather
A Praise, unto this universall Father;

10

Hee rules the ruleing Monarch's, of the Earth,
    And Peasants poore;
The crawling Emmets, have from him their Store,
    Lions their Birth;
The Royall Eagle flyes, but by his might;
And Hee secures the Sillie sparrowes flight.

11

The mightie Cedar, getts from him his Sap;
    ·And Shrubs, their Juice;
The Rose and Lillie flourish, by his Deawes;
    Nettles, by hap
Come not to seed, but by the Influence
Which He, to everie Creature, doth dispence.

ODE XIII

1

Soe powerfull, Nature doth in Things appeare,
    To this Great Rectors will;
Some things live but a Day, and some a yeare;
    Some, many years fullfill;
Some, which in Nature were thought strong enough,
        Doe soone Decaye;
        And the weake Spray,
Which yeilds to everie wind, is sometimes tough.

2

The long-lived Raven, sometime knowes a Date
    Short, as the Sparrowes Life;
The Stagge, and Sheepe may be co-terminate,
    In Natures finall Strife;
The mightie Elephant, and Mouse may run
        An Equall race;

And in this case,
The Heliotrope, may live with the last Sun.

3

That wonder: is it Natures? that a Flower
    Observing all his path,
Should change the Station, with Him everie Howre,
    And feele a kind of Death,
When his Flame quencht, to westerne waves, doth fall;
    Againe inspired,
    When he is fired,
When in his South he rides, dispred most of All:

4

Or, be it Natures worke; who gave her Power?
    The word is the mistake;
You call it Nature; but I call it more;
    That which did Nature make.
For what is Nature? but the Creature All
    Sealed by his hand;
    And cannot Stand
Without his ayde, nor yet without Him fall;

5

For not the Elements, whereby wee live,
    Can challenge ought, in this.
Hee made them Strong, or wasting; he did give
    The breath, which still is His,
To everie Creature; Soe that wee can find
    Noe Shape at all
    For what wee call
Nature, but his Impression in the Kind.

6

Thus I agree; and thus I dare avow
    Nature, our Strongest Light;

For the Thing men call Art, I do not know
     A Thing more Sleight;
For what bold Impudence, dare boast a Trade?
       Or undertake
       More strong to make
The Creature, the Creator perfect made?

7

This mightie Idoll, which fond Men adore,
     Is but a Shadow vaine;
Boasting of Knowledge, knoweing nere the more;
     But makes an Easie, plaine
Path, intricate and rugged; to invite
       By silken Clue
       Such, as pursue
Her winding Steps, to an Eternall night.

8

The Knowledge men would know; if they could tell
     What their owne thoughts would know;
Is natures Patent, Stampt with Heavens Great Seale;
     Which well surveigh'd, will Show
Large Misterie; and Misterie unfold;
       Then doe not Strive
       (Fond men) to give
Your Freedome to a Zanie, blind and bold.

9

It is the great Imposture of the world;
     A Snare, to ruine Sence;
A pitt, where glorious witts have often hurl'd
     Their brightest Excellence;
Where Sober Knowledge, and the Light of Truth
       Were never heard:

St. 8 owne thoughts]; *thoughts* has apparently been written over *Soules* in Ms.; Grosart prints both words.

But Hee, who rear'd
His Follie loudest, with a high-rais'd mouth.

10

And doubtles, thus the Earth, with Jove made warre:
    When man shall undertake
To Circle mightie Nature, in the Sphere
    Which groveling Fancies make;
What is it, This? but to their power, to raise
    A mound, to Scale
    The Olimpicke wall,
And deprive the Creator of his praise?

11

But Mightie Nature, (provident in All)
    Did this of old foresee;
And sett before the Face of Truth, a wall,
    Beyond Discoverie;
Lest man, too bold, in veiwing her bright Shine,
    Might proudlie vant
    Hee did not want
Of the Perfection justly called Devine.

12

Soe fell the Angells; soe did Man, at first
    And soe doth often fall;
For soe bold Crime, how justlie was Hee curst?
    Who seeking, lost it All;
And if there be a parcell, of that Fire,
    Not yet put out,
    It is, noe doubt
From the first Flame, who gave it first entire.

ODE XIV

1

Nothing in Nature, can be certaine fixt,
    But to the movers will;
All varie; in their Motions, strangelie mixt.
    Nothing but changeth Still;
    And what wee 'count in Nature monstrous
        Is nothing lesse;
        It is, to us;
    But is a true production, to expresse
The Maker infinite, to noe rules Tyed;
And tis his Power, to be Diversifyed.

2

Is there a certaine growth, in any Tree?
    Or Shrub, or humble plant?
Are wee made Judges, which most perfect be,
    Or which, perfection want?
    Shall wee assume unto the giddie Sence
        What is beyond
        All the pretence
Of humane Reason certainlie to find!
Perhaps the crooked Hawthorne (to the Eye
Of Nature) is as right as Cedars high.

3

Tis the same hand, which clad the blushing Rose,
    Which did the Henbane dresse;
The fragrant violet, by his bountie growes
    And loathsome weeds, noe lesse;
    Hee makes the various Tulip, please the Eye,
        And yet his Care
        Doth not denye
    To the poore Dazie, happilie as deare:
And sure, the vulgar Marigold may Cope
In Nature, with the famed Heliotrope.

4

Nor did he bid, what wee account most faire:
    The Apple, Plumme, or Grape
Be cherisht more, in Natures equall Care,
    Then her less-valued Heape;
    The Crab, and Sloae he doth alike protect;
        Nor brambles base
        Doth he neglect;
But as the supreme Rector in Each place
Doth the whole Creature, with his bountie fill:
Thus Nature is Expression of his will.

5

How is a Camel better, in his Shape,
    Then the despised Gnat?
Why doe wee wonder at the Mimicke Ape,
    Or the Rude Parrot's chat?
    The Squirrel is as worthy; and the wren
        A better note.
        Is not the Hen
And her brave Husband, in his golden Coat,
Fair, as the Phasiant? or in Natures Eyes
Perhaps as dear, as Birds of Paradice?

6

The Sea of Water, cannot onlie boast;
    Nor doth his hand Sustaine
Onlie great Rivers; or the great ones most;
    For Hee who guides the maine
    Is the same Providence to the least Spring;
        Not only Thames,
        But where I sing
    The fameles Devia, equall bountie claimes:
There will I shade my browes, and bring a Store
Of better verse, to Sing his wonders ore.

ODE XV

1

Unsatisfyed with Earth
(Where Greife, and thousand Troubles intermixe
With some poor seeming Mirth)
I put on wings; and mounting higher, fixe
On fairer objects. See the great
Rector of nature, and the universe
His gifts disperse,
In everie kind; and all his bounties meet
To make a Harmonie compleat.

2

This Power, which Nature rules,
And the whole world, is the great God of Power;
The God, which antique Schooles
Have aymed at; the God which wee Adore;
Whose Misterie, Stupendious height
Includes; the object of our Faith alone;
For he were none,
If Reason could unfold him, to our Sight;
And to fraile Sence, display that Light.

3

Oh Infinite! beyond the Quill
Of nature, or her Servant, to display;
Whose Power, is but to will
To whom the Earth, the Sea, and Heavens obay.
How shall I dare, to bring a verse
Before thy Throne of Glorie? Oh, despise
Not what shall rise
From a full Soule; though Sinfull Lips reherse
The Tenor; doe not shut thy Ears.

4

Oh, doe not shut thy Ears,
Offended with my Song; but let my Zeale

Thy Anger and my Fears
Prevent; let thy indulgent Mercie heale
The boyling ulcer, of my Sin;
And yet in Time, repaire the Soon-decay
Of thy wrought Clay.
A despised Shred of mankind, who has bin
Made clean before, Oh, cleanse agin.

5

Then will I bring to thee
My Himnes of Praise; and Celebrate thy Name;
In the best Poesie
My humble Thoughts, or Zealous fires can frame;
This, all the Tribute I can bring;
And though it be above all Taske, of verse,
I must reherse
Something to thee: the widdow can but fling
Her mites, nor I alas, but Sing.

6

Naught have I else to give;
Nor can I give it; onlie thine repay
Whose breath, first made me Live;
And gave me Being, in noe obscure way;
Noe vegetable Plant, nor Beast,
But noblest of thy Creatures, made me man,
And Christian;
Borne in the Light of Truth, where glories feast
The Soule, in Sempeternall Rest.

7

Thou, hast redeemed Mee
From double Death, and the Strict covenant
Is cancelled by thee;
Wee have a freedome, which old Times did want;
Thou hast secured me, from the wombe
Unto this Minute; that I now may praise

For all the Dayes
I have compleated, and the Time to come,
Thy mercie, to the Tombe.

8

Then let my Quill Aspire
In mightie Numbers; and thy mercies Sing
A Himne, the Soule to fire
In joyfull Rapture. Oh, could frailtie bring
Those liveing heights of Poesie,
Which Fancie faine would flatter witt into,
Here they might flow;
But wee are Silent; all our Streames are Drye;
Our Quills are Stopt, or Idlye lye.

9

Yet, will I once assay,
To honour thee, in Straines of humble Rhime;
Suffice it, if I pay
A gratefull Tribute. Hee, who guides the Time,
Expects from man, some howers t'applye
His worke: indeed his owne; for what wee give
To him, shall live
Our richest Store, when our fraile Bodies Dye,
And in the Grave, forgotten lye.

ODE XVI

1

Now faire and Cleare; the Heavens are pleas'd to Smile;
The purged Ayre doth rise
Full, in her Balme and Spice;
Spiknard and Cassia breath, to reconcile
Opposed Elements; Aurora faire
Spreads all the Treasure of her haire,
T'envite the Active Phebus more away,
And glad the Creatures, in a well-come day.

2

The night is fled; and Dayes best Chorister
    Kickes his feild-Bed with Scorne;
    In livelie Rapture, borne
To those Etheriall Courts of wonder; where
    His Liricke notes, left fyled,
    Preserved are, unsoyled;
The Royall Eagle, in the welkin towers,
And for his prey, with mightie pineon Scowers.

3

The manly Cocke, has long his Bugle Shrilled;
    And thriftie villagers
    Have long since shaked their Ears;
Each busie, in the Labour he is Skill'd;
    Their frugall wives Assay
    The offices of Day.
The night-pent flockes unbound, spread ore the Hills,
And Coridon, their Swaine, his loud Pipe Shrills.

4

Only I slug it: with a careles Head;
    And my free Genius Steepe,
    In the wide Gulph, of Sleep;
And loose my Spirrits in a tempting Bed;
    My Limbes, unapt to use,
    And all my Joyes, my Muse
Forgot in Slumbers; and my heavie Eyes,
Invite fresh Dreames: I have noe will to rise.

5

Yet, let not vertue leave me; I will Shake
    Those fetters into Ayre:
    And my quicke Thought prepare,
For free and active Rapture; I will make
    Rich nature open All
    Her treasures, which shall fall

A harvest, to enrich my sober Quill;
And purged Ears, with gratefull Accents fill.

6

Forsake me, you Dull ministers of Sleepe,
      And let me Raise my Quill,
      To Court th' Olimpicke Hill
With Earlie praises; and Survay the Heape
      Of natures bounties; then
      If I (soe bold) may Pen
Something to praise Him, whom I most admire,
My God, my Glorie, I have my Desire.

ODE XVII

      1

      When I would bring
      One verse, to Sing
    Thy Name; how Dull am I?
      Should I reherse
      Some toy in verse,
My giddie Fancie then would flye.
      Wretch that I am! how glad
      I am, of this poore trade,
      This Sillye Rime!
      Yet when I would endeavour
      To Celebrate the giver
      In a well weighd
Judicious Poesie; how lesse Sublime
      My numbers move, then ever.

      2

      When I my Clod
      Would kicke; oh God,
    How am I fettered;

St. 1 Wretch]; Wretc'h Ms.

At either heele,
(Me think's) I feele
A plummet, heavier far, then Lead;
Or like the Falcon, knit
Unto the Perch, I flitt
And make a bayte;
I picke my Jesses, and assay
For Libertie in everie way,
But cannot hitt.
I toyle and flutter; faine would breake the grate,
Where I am mewed, of Clay.

3

I may Sometime
In halfe a Rime
Hop from the Turfe; but when
I would attempt
A ravishment,
T'enrich my drye, and drousie pen;
Check'd by my bonds, I fall,
And lime my Selfe in all
The muite, and Slime.
The more I would Aspire,
The more (Alas) I tire;
Enforc'd to call
My Clog to be my Stay; and pant a Time
Upon my Bed of mire.

4

Poore helples Man,
What number Can
Expresse thy weaknesse? had
All Quills bene bent
To this intent,
How were it more then yet a Shade?
There is a Dismall Screene

Of Earth, and Sin, betweene
Us and the bright
Objects, wee would discerne.
How farre are wee to learne
The yet unknowne
Beauties of Truth? and onlye hope a Light
For which our Bowells yerne?

5

Leave me awhile,
Officious Quill;
For I have a great Thought
Unformed yet;
Nor can I fitt
It to the better Formes I ought.
Let me a while retire,
Till, warmed with Sacred Fire,
My Active nerves
Secure a stronger flight,
To gather, (from that Light
Which I admire)
Some ray; (alas) till then the Sinner Sterves,
In a Sad winters night.

ODE XVIII

1

Thus wee deceive ourselves: and Everie Day
Creates another hope; as wee might Say,
Time is not ripe, when our Time flyes away.

2

Weere but to morrow come, or next Day, here
Wee should be happie; or some seaven yeare
Hence, weele have Peace, and dwell noe more in Feare.

3

How hardly are wee pleas'd; how less content
In present fortunes? and wee still prevent
Our Joyes, in Expectation of Event.

4

One Day's too long; another is too Short;
Winter is Cold; Summer, unfitt for Sport;
The Spring is bitter, and the Autumne, Smart.

5

But for the frost, (God knowes) what wee'd ha' done;
Now wee crye out of Raine; and now the Sun
Shines too, too hot, when other fault is none.

6

What wee'd have done! if this Thing had not bene;
Still one mischance, or other, comes betweene
Us and our Hopes; or else, the world had seene

7

A Trophie, to convince Posteritie
Of our great Diligence, and Industrie,
Our Prudence, Justice, and our Pietie.

8

But ah! wee are not happie; never since
Some Day of Fate, (as we would make pretence)
Has the same Starre, had his owne Influence.

9

Oh God, how mad are men! and I not lesse
Then he the maddest; in the emptines
Of Hope, I loose my Youth, I must confesse;

10

And Delatorie Causes, still invent
To my owne prejudice; in the intent
I would pursue, most to my owne content,

11

Else why should I, this Day, my Quill forbeare?
Noe Day, noe Line; but in the Kalender
This is a Day, though shortest in the yeare;

12

And am I therfore tyed, (because the Sun
Is not with us Eight howers) to leave undone
The Dayes worke? for a morne, or Afternoone?

13

Such Students are too regular; and make
A Toyle of their Endeavours; let them take
Their nine for bed-time, and their five to wake.

14

Such method, yet I know not; though I be
A bed at Ten, I tarrie up till three
Next morning; then I watch as much as Hee;

15

For tis nor Day, nor night, nor any Time,
That can Deterre a Muse, in the sublime
Raptures of Fancie; had I now a Rhime

16

Of worth, and price; this short Decembers Day
I would spin out, to make my Readers say,
Long Barnabie was never halfe soe Gay.

ODE XIX

1

I doe not feele the Storme,
Which vexes you, in the too soone Decay
Of your fair gardens verdure. Where noe Spray
Lookes green, noe Flower
But run into his root;
Your fruit trees lower;
You cannot set your foot
In all your Garden on a liveing worme.

2

The glorie of your Toyle,
The high-pris'd Tulip, has noe Colour now;
The Gilly-flowers are dead; the Rose can show
Nor Red, nor Smell,
T'envite the willing Sence.
Who now can tell,
The violets residence?
The Sweet briar drye, the Lillie has noe foyle.

3

When I, beyond the Rage
Of Time, or winters malice, now can Show
A liveing Paradice; and lead you, through
Greene Alleys, set
With ever verdant flowers;
The violet
Wants odour, to the worst of ours;
Trim Nature stands here, in firme Equipage.

4

I have a Rose, will keepe
Its Scent, and beautie, to another Spring;
(Nor wonder that I say it) I can bring
This verie Day,

(Dead winter haveing nipt
Yours into Clay)
A goodly Tulip, Stript
In Gold and Purple; Nature not asleepe.

5

How doe they drop away?
Your flowers, and Joyes together? Goe with me
Into Apolloes Garden; you shall see,
To mocke at yours
And frustrate all your Thought,
A bed of Flowers,
Into quaint mazes wrought;
The Muses bower, under the liveing Bay.

ODE XX

1

What mad men are wee, of the versing trade?
To give our witt
To Everie Censure? And noe doubt
A Thousand, to the Common Eye has Strayed
Ere one has hit;
And us the workmen, fooles, they flout.

2

An Epicke is too grave; a Satire Sharpe.
Sonnet is Light;
Elegie Dull; in Epigram
Wee want our Salt; and Ignorance will carpe,
Although we write
A Region, beyond All they claime.

3

Yet Silly men are wee; and here I should
Desist, from all

My Exercise of witt; if sure
I knew an able Judge to read, that could
But Errors call
Which Errors were, and know whats pure.

4

I durst not put my witt, unto the Test
Of such a Man;
I find a guilt, with my owne Eyes,
A partiall Father; yet not soe possest
Of my owne braine
But I can see Deformities;

5

Perhaps a fault, where the good Reader huggs
My verie Name;
And let him Joy, in all he found;
Where I am proud of witt, perhaps he Shruggs,
And Sighes, tis Lame;
Soe 'twer, if I to him were bound.

6

But let me give Advice: doe not pretend
To judge of witt;
It is an Emmett in a Cloud;
And you have but dimme Eyes: my honest freind.
If wee Submitt,
Your Sence may make this Ant, a Toade.

7

Then will I not sitt downe, with this Rebuke;
But once againe
Joy, with the Muses; innocent
In my designe; adventuring to looke
In noe mans braine
For witt, beyond his Argument.

St. 5 Reader huggs] Grosart; Readers huggs Ms.

ODE XXI

1

When Ease and Sleepe, the busye world has husht;
And Sixe howers cold, the Sun our Hemisphere
      Has left in Darke;
I, with the Muses Joy, and freely there,
Expostulate my Fancies, to the Just
      Ayme of their marke.

2

A Thousand objects, flitt within my braine;
Some slip, as shadowes; some like Columnes stand
      To fixe upon;
Which I survay, and with a serious hand
Delineate; cheiflie to entertaine
      My selfe alone.

3

And though my Body hardly well allowes
These frequent watchings; I am soe much wed
      To my Delight;
When Ease and Health, would move me to my bed,
And (free from guilt) with unperplexed browes,
      Might sleepe, the Night;

4

Yet rather Chuse I, to my Healths impaire,
With gentle Muses, to bestow my Time
      In the weake blaze
Of a Sad Lampe; and free from greater Crime,
Sing to my selfe, the Fancies I prepare,
      A Thousand waies.

5

And I will Sing great Things; perhaps to please
The Judging Reader; and to pussle those
      Who pretend more.

But Stay; my carefull Leech noe more allowes,
Checks my Disorder; and has stay'd to dresse
    Mee, a long Hower;

6

For, I must now observe Him; but when Time
M' imposthum'd members, shall againe make light,
    I will be free,
In midnight Revels to the Appetite
Of my owne Genius in the purest Rhime
    And Poesie.

ODE XXII

1

Cleare, as untroubled waters from their Spring,
And pure, as Innocence her Selfe can Sing,
    Modest, as virgin Brides;
    Whose gentle blushings, hides
What they expresse; Sweet, as the blooming Rose:
Faire, as the Earlie Morning, when she Showes
    Her golden Face, and Deawie Lockes doth tye
    In azure Fillets: Such be my Poesie;

2

Not bound to flatter Titles; or let loose
To vulgar passions, in the Times abuse;
    Not limited; not Free
    Further then modestie
Can warrant, in Each Syllable; not led
To Sooth opinion; neither soe much wed
    To my owne Sence, but I all formes may See
    In proper orbes: Such be my Poesie.

3

Such be my Poesie: that number may
In Clear expressions, all my Thoughts display;

Such Rapture fill my Thought,
As I may utter nought,
Beneath the dignitie, of a free Muse;
And guided, by my Genius, Chuse
Objects sublime; adoreing God, the high
Author of Truth: such be my Poesie.

ODE XXIII

1

Poore bird, I doe not envie thee;
Pleas'd, in the gentle Melodie
Of thy owne Song.
Let crabbed winter Silence all
The winged Quire; he never shall
Chaine up thy Tongue.
Poore Innocent,
When I would please my selfe, I looke on thee;
And guess some sparkes, of that Felicitie,
That Selfe Content.

2

When the bleake Face, of winter Spreads
The Earth, and violates the Meads
Of all their Pride;
When Saples Trees, and Flowers are fled
Backe, to their Causes; and lye dead
To all beside;
I see thee Sett,
Bidding defiance, to the bitter Ayre;
Upon a wither'd Spray, by cold made bare,
And drooping yet.

3

There, full in notes, to ravish all
My Earth, I wonder what to call
My dullnes; when

I heare thee, prettye Creature, bring
Thy better odes of Praise, and Sing
To pussle men.
Poore pious Elfe!
I am instructed, by thy harmonie,
To sing away, the Times uncertaintie,
Safe in my Selfe.

4

Poore Redbrest, caroll out thy Laye
And teach us mortalls what to saye.
Here cease, the Quire
Of ayerie Choristers; noe more
Mingle your notes; but catch a Store
From her Sweet Lire;
You are but weake,
Meere summer Chanters; you have neither wing
Nor voice, in winter. Prettie Redbrest, Sing
What I would speake.

ODE XXIV

1

It is Enough to me,
If I her Face may see;
Let others boast her Favours, and pretend
Huge Interests; whilst I
Adore her Modestie;
Which Tongues cannot deprave nor Swords defend;

2

For could She Fall,
To what we call
Censure; how weake and vulgar were her Fame?
Not Ignorance would hold

St. 3 sing away, the Times] Ms.; sing the Time's Grosart.

Till his long Tale were told;
Though scarcelie he, has ever heard her Name.

3

If wee might read
Her truly Charactred,
It were enough, Error to vindicate,
To warme the Stupid wretch,
(Who onlie lives, to stretch
His frozen nerves) with Rapture, 'bove his Fate.

4

But while I bring
My verse, to Sing
Her Glories, I am strucke with wonder, more;
And all the Formes, I see,
But Emptie Shadowes bee,
Of that Perfection which I adore.

5

Be silent then,
All Tongues of men,
To Celebrate the Sex; for if you fall
To other Faces, you
Wander, and but pursue
Inferior objects; weake, and partiall.

ODE XXV

1

My Dear Pudora, though the greedie Flame
    Has Swallowed all the Inke
Which I (the weake Adorer of thy name)
    Once lavisht out, yet thinke
        A second Store,
Tooke, from thy Graces, may to better Light
Celebrate thee; I am not bankrupt Quite;
        And were I poore
To the Extreame of Ignorance, that Fire
Still liveing, in your Eyes would Heat inspire.

2

Doe not; oh doe not, (Goddes of my Muse)
    Thinke I have lost, that Zeale
My former Quill profest; nor thinke I chuse
    Of lower Things to tell;
        Forbid it, all
My better Fate. Noe; rather may I pine
In my owne Joy, my verse, if my designe
        Did ever fall
Unto another object; but I still
Steer'd by your Eyes; Starrs, to direct my Quill.

3

Nor blame some looser Sheets; if (when I lackt
    Your Light) my verse might Stray
From the precise Path, which your Steps had track't;
    I cannot, dare not Say,
        But I have gone
Sometimes aside; yet take, in leiu of All
My follies, this Acknowledgment: tis small
        The wrong, I ha' done;

St. 1 bankrupt]; banrupt Ms.: ban'rupt Grosart.

Pardon, where I Nicotiana Sung,
And I dare say, I never did you wrong:

4

For though, in Silvia, I my selfe might please;
    Twas but at once, to bring
Under that name, a double Species;
    And where I loudest Sing,
        With all my Praise,
To honour Her, I but derive a Sparke
From your more radiant Flame, which is the marke,
    Of all my Bayes;
But Shee, revolted like her Selfe, can claime
Nothing in all my Poesie, but name.

5

This may Suffice. Great Rectres of my Thought,
    Daigne once againe, to smile
On my Endeavours; and I will not doubt
    To vindicate our Ile,
        From all the blast
Of Envie, or Detraction; I will raise
Huge Monuments of wonder; manye-wayes
    Which shall outlast
The rage of Time, and stand the Boast of Fame;
My verse Eternized, in Pudoraes name.

ODE XXVI

1

How am I lost! though some are pleas'd to say
    My mossy Chops, estrange
All former Knowledge; and my Brother may
    At distance interchange
Discourse, as to a man, he nere had knowne.

It cannot be; perswade
Your Selves; for when you made
Me take a Glass, I knew my Face, my owne;

2

The verie Same I had, three years agoe;
My Eye, my Lip, and nose,
Little, and great, as then; my high-slick't Brow,
Not bald as you suppose;
For though I have made riddance, of that Haire,
Which full enough did grow,
Cropt, in a Zealous bow
Above each Eare, these but small Changes are;

3

For wer't my worke, I need not farre goe seeke
The Face I had last yeare;
The groweing Frindge, but swept from either Cheeke,
And I as fresh appeare
As at nineteene; my Perruke, in as neat
An Equipage, as might
Become a wooer, light
In thoughts, as in his Dresse; but I forget,

4

Or rather I neglect, this Trim of Art;
And have a Care soe small,
To what I am, in any outward part,
I scarce know one of All;
Tis not that Forme, I looke at. Could I find
My inward Man, compleat
In his Dimensions, let
Mee glorie Truth; the better part's behind.

DANIEL IN BEARD

ODE XXVII

1

Soe should you have my Picture. Would it change
    And varie, to the Time;
      But when I see
Art permanent, and nature fade, how Strange
    Would it appear to me?
      And twitt my Slime
As weake materialls, to the Painters stuffe;
There youthfull Still, in my Selfe, bald, or rough,
      With Age, and Time enough.

2

Twould trouble me; when I with frosted hairs,
    Should looke, at what I was;
      And see my selfe
Sanguine and fresh; my Eyes there quicke and Cleare;
    And I, a Sordid Elfe.
      What a sweet Glasse
Were this, to make me mad? and love againe
My youthfull Follies; and but change the Straine,
      Doating, for Light and vaine?

3

Noe; would you see me better, you who presse
    To have my Picture tooke,
      Beyond all Art;
I leave it here, my selfe; it will expresse
    More then the formall looke
      Or outward part;
A better draught, I leave you; doe not Strike
My Feature, to the Cunning of Van Dyke;
      This, this is farre more like.

4

Here looke upon me, as I am in Truth;
    Let everie Leafe present

Some severall part;
And draw em into forme: to the just growth
Of my intendement;
To pussle Art,
In her loud boast, and something leave behind
Unto my Freinds; that whosoe lookes, may find
The Effigies of my Mind:

5

And though perhaps, the Colours are but poore;
And some defects appeare
To the strict Eye;
You will not Censure, want of Cunning more,
To pourtray Truth, if I
Have bristlie haire,
Or my head bald, or beard in Cop'ses grow.
Will Art soe trim me, that they must not show?
Who then my Face, could know?

6

Had I bene more exact, I had bene lesse;
And though I might have put
More varnish on,
It had bene Time ill spent; and might expresse
More fine proportion;
But without doubt,
Lesse to the Life; and I would now appeare
In my Just Symmetrie; though plaine, yet Cleare.
Soe, may you see me here.

ODE XXVIII
1
What a Strange Thing is Man?
How weake, in his Designe,
His Wisedome? for I can

See others now in mine;
How Dull? how lost
To what he Studied most?

2

Wee cannot looke upon
Our inwarde selves, but find
Man generall; for one
Is all, and everie Mind;
In some Degree
Seeing our Selves, wee others see.

3

The same, our Common Cares,
Our Passions, are alike;
Our causles Hopes, and Fears
At the same objects strike;
And all our Store
Of Follies, less or more.

4

Our Frailties, our desires,
Our Policies, our Plots,
Are fed from Common Fires;
Not wisedome, in her knots,
But cunning hands
May by his owne, loose others bands.

5

This Image, which wee reare
Unto our Selves, is not
Soe radiant, and Clear
As wee suppose; the lot
Is free to All;
And diverse things, by the same name, we call.

ODE XXIX

1

This Dullnes is improper to the Day,
And I am Sad; not in a common way;
    My Fancie, Darke as night,
    And fixed; all the Light
        Of Reason fled;
        And I am dead
    Unto my selfe; I seeke
    A Thousand waies, to breake
The Cloud which doth involve me; and invade
With a strange mist, the little light I had.

2

I cannot speake, what I would strive to say;
And what I most would doe, I most delay;
    I doe not know my Thought;
    Or rather I thinke nought
        Which can be knowne;
        I'me not my owne
    Disposer to the poore
    Follies of everie howre;
And common Things, I can noe more intend,
Then grave Designes; but from all purpose bend.

3

How am I Stupid? how below my thought?
Am I to Sottishnes, and nothing, brought?
    I doe not breath, as once;
    But closed in Ignorance
        I seeme to dwell,
        As in a Shell;
    Where my close-breathing tires
    My Lungs, in oft respires;
And fainting, all my Spirrits loose their use;
Why am I choack'd? why am I stifled thus?

ODE XXX

1

The Sprightlie Larke, upon yond Easterne Hill,
          His early vowes
Has payed; and summons up my Lazy Quill
          Againe to rouse,
And in Cleare notes, like her owne Harmonie,
          Salute the Day;
          But I, Dull Sinner, Stay,
And her third Himne performed. How dull am I?

2

The golden beames, of bright Apollo long
          Has warmed the Earth,
And got his morning draught; I have a Tongue,
          And noe such Dearth
Of Fancie, to be meerlie silent, when
          All Creatures bring
      Somewhat, for offering.
Why should I sleepe? or not enlarge my Pen?

3

It were but soe; had still the Power of Ice
          In Ebon walls,
It Pris'ner kept; I will awake, arise.
          When Vertue calls,
Shame were it, to prefer a Pillow, soft
          With Ease and Sin
        To her resplendent Shine.
I better Feathers take, and mount aloft.

4

Emulous of the Larke, in her uprise,
          And in her Song,
I quitt this dunghill Earth; let it suffice
          If I, among

The other Creatures, a small Tribute bring;
    One verse, or note,
  Though from a harsher throte.
The poore wren Cherups, what the Larke doth Sing.

5

In a Consort of Praise, all Creatures joyne;
    The Squallid owle
Twitters a midnight note; though not soe fine,
    Yet with a Soule
As gratefull, as the Nightingales cleare Song;
    The universe
  Doth the great Himne reherse.
I only bear my part, the rest among.

6

Then, with fresh Pineons drest, I will assay
    My part to raise,
And celebrate his name, who to this Day
    Hath many waies
Preserved me. Oh god, I have a Quill,
    Muddled, and lame,
  To magnifie thy name.
Asham'd, I lay it by; I've done soe much, soe ill.

ODE XXXI

1

Welcome my Lampe awhile;
I may enjoy thy oyle
Without Disturbance; and allay
The foule distempers of the Day,
With sober recreations, of the Night;
All Eyes are closed, of Ignorance and Spight;
For it is late;

My watch doth prate
Of twelve or one. Deare Muses, wee may yet
Solace an howre; for ever may he gett
　　The name of Sluggard, who doth grutch
　　A midnight hower, for witt too much.
　　　　For me, I would allow
　　　　All time, one day to yow.

　　2

　　　　Yet, rather let us keepe
　　　　Our howers; and mocke at Sleepe;
　　For safest, when the Sun is downe,
　　From noise and Croud, wee are our owne;
Nor yet auspicious Phebus, can produce
Effects more glorious, from the lab'ring Muse,
　　　　Then Luna pale;
　　　　Noe idle tale
Of giddie wits perplex her serious howers;
Noe loud day Noises, when the Cittie doores
　　Are all lockt up; but onlie such
　　As ever have a Key, too much.
　　　　Shee takes her wing; but stay,
　　　　The Cocke has summon'd Day.

ODE XXXII
　　　1

　　　　Are onlie Poets mad?
　　　　Tis an unluckie trade;
　　Our moderne, and the old Democritus,
　　Saw all the world, were Lunatickes with us;
　　　　And if I (partiall) may
　　　　The present Age survay;
　　　　　I am afraide
Wee are not onlie, or not the most mad.

2

See, to the Politicke;
Is not Hee partly Sicke?
Are his Designes unmixt with Drosse, and Loame?
Has he not some respects, he brought from home?
Are all his Counsells weighd?
His Actions ballanced
Within the right
Skale of cleare Judgment, and not one found light?

3

See all the world unfram'd,
Strangelie disjoynted, lamed;
And Common Men, (who have noe project, to
Advance their Fortunes) run a madding too;
Sneake in their Follies; pyre
At madnes, Misterie;
And we may See
The infection spread to All, in some degree;

4

Not least, where often, most
Sound Faculties they boast.
This saw, of old, much seeing Lucian;
And tis but now the same; for everie Man
Is bound, to his owne heart;
Not blanching any part
Of his owne Sence;
And strives to guild, all Follie with pretence.

5

The learning of the time
Is sicke; and the Sublime
Notions of men are sunke; our Industrye
(Not meerlie simple) has its Subtletye;
All men, have in their waies

Distraction; Pride, and Praise,
Makes the world mad.
The Poet sings, the Polititian's Sad.

.

ODE XXXIII

1

Oh, doe not breath too loud; though greife sometimes
In rude Expressions, and disordred Rhimes
Appeare;
It is not safe to sigh too loud, when wee
Deplore such tender Cases; Poesie
Must here
Curbe her free Quill; and couch a big intent
In the darke folds, of a faigned Argument.

2

But Danger, onlie guilt attends; I bring
White Thoughts; and never learned how to sing
Of more
Then Truth and Justice in each Line might seale;
Unbyassed with Spleene, or too much Zeale.
How poore
Should I my selfe account? had I bene swaied
By these fraile Passions, this, or that t' have said?

3

Then may I boldly utter, my free Thought;
And to the Age, poure all my Bosome out.
I will
Noe longer Swell, and pinch my throbbing brest
With Fears and Fancies, to my owne unrest.
Poor Quill!
Yet thou art free, and Just to all my Care;
I am befreinded Still, to have thee neare.

4

And though perhaps, I privilie expresse
The summe of all my Thoughts, when nothing lesse
            Is read;
I write what I intend, and rather Chuse
Such Intricacies; though not soe abtruse
            As need
An Index, to informe me what the Ayme
Was, when I laied the plott, or raised the frame.

ODE XXXIV

            It is not worth your Care:
My better Poem's, which the greedie Flame
Devour'd. Tis true; they might have kept my name,
            More glorious, and faire
Unto Posteritie, then I can hope
From these remaining Trifles; and perhaps
Have given a Light to those, who can but grope
The way, and Stumble; or surprised, in Trapps
Of Cunning, fall to Ruine; this, and more,
            They might have done;
            But I am one
Who value nothing of my private Store.
Who knowes! but they determin'd were, to fall,
Part of a greater Ruine? and unfitt
To give such Light to future Times, as shall
Brand our owne Age in witt, for want of witt?
            I doe not yet despaire
When silver-winged Peace againe shall Shine,
To raise a Poesie, in everie Line,
            As high, as full, as faire.

ODE XXXV

1

Poor Clod of Earth, Despise
Thy Slime; and yet be wise.
Thou art unable, to attaine
That Pitch;
And knowing it, not to refraine
Were madnes; yet desist;
Though with a greedy fist,
And Itch,
Thou covet it. Leave of to clime
That Hill, which will upbraid thy Time.

2

Though fired with glorie; all
Motives of Honour, call
Thee up to this sublime Endeavour;
Yet know,
The golden Anadem is never
Designed for thy head;
A Thousand, thousand, led
As thou
With selfe-surmises; yet appeare
Examples, others to deterre.

3

And though the Goale were won
Thou dost propose, undone
Were yet the greater worke; it is
Beyond
Thy manage, were it taught; to this
My feeble Lampe, as much
Might fire Heavens greatest Brouch;
And find
Perpetuall Fuell, to Adorne
Th' Horizon, better then the Morne.

4

Away! presumptuous wretch;
Tis set beyond thy reach;
With humble Admiration, fall
And kisse
Thy mother Earth: farewell to all
Thy follies bid, and see
Its state, and thy degree;
Soe misse
Thy certaine ruine. Soe the Sun
Wee see best, in reflection.

5

Invert thy Eyes; and see
Its State, and thy degree,
Where many formes appeare; and all
The hid
Causes in Nature, rise, or fall,
To what wee apprehend,
Which is not true; unbend
That thred
Of Fancie, knit before; and See,
Truth onlie meets Humilitie.

ODE XXXVI

1

Huge weight of Earth, and Sin;
Which clogs my lab'ring Thoughts, in their uprise;
I am not wise
Enough to breake my Chaine, or cast my Skin
With prudent Adders; could I slip
From my old Slime, how would I skip!
In my new Robes, of Innocence and veiwe
Things in their Causes, absolute and true.

2

Then, in a scornfull heat,
And brave Disdaine, enfranchis'd would I flye,
To kisse that Skye,
Wee now admire; and find a fixed Seat
Above the lower Region, where
Th' attractive Earth, I need not feare;
But move without my Load, and at one Step
As eas'ly mount the orbe, as downward leape.

3

There could I see, and scorne
The busie toyle of Mankind, in their waies;
Their nights, and Dayes,
How fruitles, to the End; as were they borne
To satisfye their Lust, and Pride,
To their owne Sence diversifyed;
And added nothing, to the gen'rall frame,
But a meer thing, put in to have a name.

4

How everie other Thing
Applies its part! and has a Motion,
Which (though unknowne)
Doubtles, it doth aright performe; and bring
Its little, to maintaine the whole:
Man onlie, who should have a Soule
More noble and refin'd, by nature made
Surveiour of the worke, doth nothing Adde.

5

Diverted from the charge,
Entrusted to him meerly: as beyond
In face and mind,
The other Creatures; with a Thought, as large
As all the orbes, and wider too;

Truth, (whose vast Circle none can know)
Was onlie bigger; and the Light of Truth,
Met full and radiant here, from North to South.

6

Thus once; but now, alas,
The most despised object of the world;
From all this hurl'd,
A Slave to Passion, and his owne disgrace;
Baited by Follie, and Surprised,
In the great Snare, which Hee devis'd
Of pleasant vanitie; and all the boast
Hee had of Dignitie and worth, is lost.

7

Poor Sand of Earth, how lost
To thy owne ruine art thou, in thy will?
And plotting Still
Further destruction! as though all were lost
Of thy Creation, in thy Selfe;
Now made a wracke, upon the Shelfe
Of Ignorance, hopest there thy selfe to Save
From utter Death, and the devouring wave.

ODE XXXVII

Looke above, and see thy wonder;
Downward looke, and see it under;
Upon thy Right hand, see it shine;
And meet thy Left, in the same Line;
Survay the Earth; and sound the deepe;
From those that flye, to those that Creepe.
See everie Creature: and behold

7　See everie] Ms.; In everie　Grosart.

From the base Mirtle, to the old
Majesticke oke; veiwe everie plant,
Herbe, root, or flower; none wonder want;   10
Consider Springs; and as you passe,
Meet wonder, in the smallest grasse;
Let even Dust, and Atomes rise
To strike new wonder, in thy Eyes;
Observe the rapid orbes; and see
A Cloud, beyond Discoverie.
See all about thee; and display
Thy understanding, to the ray
Of this combined Flame; this tongue
Of universall praise, has sung   20
To a Deafe Eare. All objects stand
To teach, but wee not understand.
Are these obscure? or too remote?
Beyond thy notion, or thy note?
Looke at thy selfe; and wonder more:
Nature contracted, in her Store.

ODE XXXVIII

1

Rapt by my better Genius; beyond
    The power of Earth I sitt;
And see all humaine follye in its kind;
    Not what wee fancie, witt,
But has its blemish there; or Arrogance,
    Or selfe opinion,
Or Impudence, or Flatterie, or Chance,
    Or blind Affection,
  Support the maine; these set away
  What common Things wee doe, or Say.

2

Poor crauling Emmetts! in what busie toyle
    Wee slip away our Time?
Our glorious Daylight, and our midnight oyle,
    Spent, to enlarge our Crime.
What a prodigious Spectacle, I veiwe!
    When I from hence looke downe,
Upon the Common Earth! which once I knew
    And made my proper owne
  With as much Zeale, as were my Fate
  Chained to the whirle of her Estate.

3

Now got above the mist, of flesh and blood,
    I am inform'd aright,
In all the Misterie, of Bad and Good:
    A never-fadeing Light
Surrounds me; that to Judge, I cannot erre.
    What have I rashly said?
Arrogant foole! my Taper went out here
    And left me, halfe dismaied
To thinke, how it a Tipe might be
Of the great Light, put out in Mee.

ODE XXXIX

1

Never to be at Ease; never to rest;
        What brest
Is strong enough? what braine? if it were double,
Could beare unmoved, the assaults of soe much trouble?
    Tost on the wave of Chance,
    I loose my better Selfe;
        Where Ignorance
        Cast up a Shelfe,
To ruine all my vertue; I forgot
My manhood, and the Treasure which I putt,
        A Sure
And constant rescue, from all hands impure.

2

Taught by Example, and the precepts, which
        From rich
Antiquitie I gathered; I was made
Fortune-proofe in her Malice; not afraide
    To cope with Danger, in
    All Formes, She could put on.
        But lost within
        Opinion,
I was surprised; and ere I could collect
Dispersed notions, by an indirect
        Strange way,
Passion prevailed. I knew not what to Say.

3

Fortified in my Reason, once I thought
        (But nought
Availes our owne Surmises) that the power
Of fortune could not Storme me. Ah, noe more
    Let womans Son be proud
    In his owne brest, or braine;

For soe I stood,
To entertaine
All hazard unappall'd; and had within
As great a Force, as full a Magazin,
As might
Have flattered you, to the Same oversight.

*   *   *   *

Man is not Strong at all, nor wise; nor Fitt
His owne to manage, with his proper witt;
Then least, when borne by Selfe-opinion,
Hee Stops the Light, and wanders in his owne
Darke Principles and notions; hee attains
Nearest Perfection, who his owne restrain's.

ODE XL

1

I cannot dwell in Sorrow; neither please
My Selfe with Shadowes, though I live at Ease.
I cannot laugh away,
The trouble of the Day;
Nor yet soe much oppress my Spright
In Tears, to linger out the Night.
I cannot make my Case,
Discourse, for everie place;
Nor meerlie rest
In my owne brest,
Silent. I am not proud in Miserie;
Nor Sordid, in my Hopes uncertaintie.

2

I cannot breake into an Extasie
Of Passion, Danted with my Miserie;
Nor make my owne Cares more

St. 1   Shadowes,] Ms.; Shadowes.   Grosart.
Ease.]; Ease;   Ms.; Ease,   Grosart.

. 136 .

Then Some have bene before;
My Sufferings are noe greater, then
The feelings of a Thousand Men,
    Perhaps as Innocent.
    Why then, should I lament
        The pettie losse
        Of goods? or drosse?
Shall these, which are but casuall, subject all
My better Treasures, to their Rise or Fall?

3

I cannot fall soe low; though I sometimes
May looke into the glasse, of these Sad Times;
    And 'mongst those Shadowes, See
    One, that resembles me,
  Naked, and nere to ruine in
  His Fortune; yet I cannot Sin
    Soe much to Providence,
    As for the pangue of Sence,
        Exclaime, and rave;
        Or wish the Grave
Might end him, with his Sorrowes; or invent
Fears to him, for a further punishment.

4

I cannot safelie looke, at my owne Sore,
Nor search too deepe, lest I should make it more;
    Soe, the unknowing Leech
    Tortures the bleeding wretch
  Under his Cure. I am not blind
  To my owne Danger; neither find
    Soe great a Burthen, in
    This miserie of mine,
        But I may Stand;
        And understand
It, as the Common Lot; by my owne Share
Soe prevent Fortune, ere She be aware.

ODE XLI

1

I doe not glorie in my Fate;
Nor prise it at an under rate;
I doe not boast
Any thing I possesse; I am not tyed
Against my Judgement, unto any Syde;
Nor am I lost,
Soe much to reason, that I chuse
Supported Error, and refuse
Neglected Truth;
Contented, to abide
Her votarie, against the vulgar mouth.

2

Let the full Pens of vanitie, Contend
In what they please;
And gaine the Ende
Of their owne seeking, humane Praise;
Lost, with the Breath wherein it straies.
I cannot fall
To flatter Pride, and Follie in her Ease;
But speake my knowledge, though it should displease
The common-Hall
Of Ignorance; and if I meet
Death, I have found my winding Sheet.

3

I am a man in everie Step
Of Life I tread; and cannot leape
Above that name;
Nor can I grovell, in a bruitish way
Lost to my nature. This is all. I say
I am that Same
Unsteddye thing, wee call a man;

St. 3   nature. This is all. I] Grosart; nature, this is all I   Ms.

. 138 .

Limited in my Selfe; and can
　　Neither deface,
　　Nor yet array,
That Image. Tis my Glorie, my Disgrace.

ODE XLII

1

Goe; make a Rape on Fancie; and bring downe
All formes, dispersed in that Region,
　　Unto our Common Light;
Then with a cunning Hand, collect the Parts,
And make a Bodie, to astonish Arts.
　　Draw your owne Face aright;
Give common man his Symmetrie, in all
　　Dimensions of the mind;
　　This were a worke, to bind
The indebted world, a Slave perpetuall.

2

But what thin Shadowes flitt, within the Braine?
What obscure notions move to entertaine
　　Men, in their owne Conceite?
Wee looke at Passions through the Subtill glasse
Of Selfe-conceit; and follow them in chase,
　　With the loud noise of witt;
Wee run our Selves aground, upon that Shelfe,
　　Our Reason bids us Shun.
　　How soone is Man undone?
Who carries his owne Ruine, in Himselfe?

3

I cannot reach, nor Span my Selfe within
My owne Dimensions; I have often bin
　　Busie, to draw my owne
To my owne Power; and with all Diligence

The dispers'd Fragments of Intelligence
    I gladlie would have knowne;
And us'd as in my Power, the Facultie
      Of everie Sence. The Reach
      Of Reason, I would fetch
Into the Circle of Capacitie.

4

I would have seen my Selfe, as in a Sheath
Within my Selfe; and as my owne, bequeath
      Each part to proper use;
My conquer'd Reason, to submit her Power.
My Sence, corrected in Exterior
      Objects, alone to chuse
What I propose; then doe not aske, what part
      I would have guide the rest;
      I would have everie brest
Capable of the rule of his owne Heart.

5

Thus, could wee Draw our Selves, the worke were done;
Knowledge were perfected; and truth were won.
      Then all our toyle had End,
Our Parts reduc'd; Each to his Station;
And wee might live, in re-Creation.
      But who shall yet ascend
That great Scientiall orbe? and bring away
      The wreath, of victorie?
      What humane Industrie,
Knowes how to Doe? what witt knowes what to Say?

ODE XLIII

1

Walke noe more, in those Sweet Shades,
Where Roses canopie your Heads;
And the fragrant violet spreads
    A purple Tapistrie;
Where all the Quire, had wont to Sing
Their earlie notes; and everie thing
Was pleasure, to entrance a King,
    Beyond his Destinie;
      Ah, now noe more
Frequent those Shades, you knew or loved before.

2

Goe, to the horrid vale of Care;
And tread the maze, of your owne Feare.
There grow noe Bayes, nor mirtles there,
    But the Sad dismall Yeiugh:
Day birds are banished this grove.
The monstrous Batt, alone doth rove;
And the dire Screich-owle, percht above
    Your over-clouded Brow
      Shall make you Sad,
Beyond the Cause of Sorrow, which you had.

3

There horrid Croakings sound; and sad
Accents of Death, untimelie made,
Rend humane Eares. Oh, Dismall Shade,
    Why am I curst? to Chuse
In thy Sad Alleyes, to weare out
My Youth? in all my Joyes forgot?
To thy unhappie walkes, I brought
    A more unhappie Muse;
      But a Muse, fitt
To joyne with thy Inhabitants; and Sitt

4

Upon the Bankes, of thy Sad Poole;
Where Frogs, and loathsome Toads doe houle;
Where all their Spaune, with yellings foule,
    Fill the corrupted Ayre.
To these, my Accents well may Suite;
My harsher grones will strike em mute;
And teach em to draw ruder out,
    Deeper, and worse by farre;
      For they are free,
Of that ranke venome which imposthumes Mee.

5

With these then, will I joyne my verse;
And everie Accent, unto theirs
Shall double grones; let me reherse
    Noe more, the tuned Lay
To liveing waters; bid Farewell
To all the Silver birds, which dwell
Upon their Streams; and never tell
    Of my owne Devia.
      Farewell to all
Wee Joy, or Peace, or Light, or Pleasure call.

ODE XLIV

    Away,
Fond man! thy braine is Sicke; thy Quill doth stray;
    There is noe Cause of Discontent,
    Soe farre should move thee, to lament;
    Distressed Fancie doth obscure
    Thy Reason, in the Calenture
      Of Passion.
    Erect thy understanding, to
    The Cause imagined, of thy woe;

Which is noe Cause, but a pretence;   10
Which Reason Sicke, unto the Sence
           Doth Fashion.
In Sober numbers, sing away
Thy Sorrowes; or at lest allay
The Apprehension of thy Ill;
    Take, take againe, thy modest Quill;
And yet retaine, the Libertie thy Muse
           Would Chuse.

ODE XLV

1

Each Day another Man; another Mind;
       And wee our Selves forget.
Chang'd in opinion; all wee left behind
       Is lost. What once was witt
            To our owne tast,
Wee relish not; but in Each newer find
       More Joy; and gladlie hast
Through Follies Zodiacke, from the first to th' Last.

2

Wearie in everie Action, wee pursue,
       Ere wee can perfect anye;
Sicke of the old, unsatisfyed with new,
       And greedie after manye;
            Never at Ease
To our owne Thoughts; and what wee ought t' eschew,
       With Scorne and Bitternes,
Wee hug, our Glorie, and grow fat in these;

3

Glad in all present madnes; and can looke
       Noe further, then the Time
Enjoyed to the purpose. Let the booke

Of Conscience babble Crime
        To the gray haire;
Whose blood is cold, and Sinnewes palsey-strooke;
        Let him grow Dead, with Feare,
And languish minutes till he meet the Beere.

4

But wee are yonge; and though wee doe not Love
        To hear our Follies read,
Wee yet Act, what wee please; and freely move
        In everie Step wee tread.
            Wee will not See
Backe, to Committed ones; nor yet reprove
        Our owne Debilitie
In the pursuit of a fresh vanitie.

5

Though I confes, when I with Judgment scan
        My Actions, and peruse
My Selfe, in all the frailtyes of a Man;
        I doe not much refuse
            To see the past
Errors of youth; and Judge em, as I can:
        Some please, and some distast;
Some I am proud of, Some away I cast.

6

Though in a rigid Sence, I must confesse
        All humane Actions are
Madnes and Follie; yet this foolishnes
        Has made me, to appeare
            To my owne Eyes,
My owne full Image; where without all dresse
        Of ornamentall Lyes,
I am not blind, to my Deformityes.

ODE XLVI

1

I grovell Still; and cannot gaine
The orbe, I flutter at in vaine;
My Thought is narrow; and my Language weake
To give my Smaller Comprehensions plaine;
 Something it is, I faine would speake;
 But as my Fancies rise, they breake.

2

Wrapt in my native weed of Sin,
I cannot cast; but search within
The folds, and would a better raiment find;
Starved in the old mantle, now worne thin.
 This beggars Coat dejects my mind,
 In all Attempts I have designed.

3

Raggs doe not fitt a Court; nor can
Man, in this Motley, meerlie man
Stand, in the privie Chamber of his heart:
Where Knowledge keeps the doore; and Truth doth raigne
 Empresse of all, and everie part
 Bound to noe Rule, nor forme of Art.

4

When I (encouraged by Some
Waiters at large) would nearer come
To wonder, at the Glorie of her State;
I sneak'd abash'd into another Roome;
 And like Court-gazers, I can prate
 Of Something seen, but know not what.

5

Thus Silly man; I am content
To get a Sight; although I went

Never beyond the Threshold, of her Court.
Enough; I thought I saw her, in her Tent,
    And guest the greatness of her Port,
    By what some others did report.

6

    But who can tell aright, her State?
    Forbid to humane Eyes? Of late
I heard, one of her nearest Servants Say:
These bold Intruders, sate without the Gate
    Ignorant gazers; and did Stay
    For Almes, there given everie Day.

7

    Then with the rest, why may not I
    Talke, of gay Sights and braverie?
To make the world esteeme me wise, and brave?
But I am Conscious; and well-pleas'd to see
    The greatest Priviledge I have,
    An equall Man, an Earthborne Slave.

ODE XLVII

1

Be not too Zealous; I ere this have seene
A Pangue as hot, a votarie as keene,
    Dye, in its height of Flame;
    Where everie word, has beene
A Panegericke; all Addresses came
To Celebrate the Glorie, of one name.

2

A Quill, inspired with noe vulgar heat,
Made great in Numbers, in his ayme more great;
    Supported in his choice;
    And honored to meete

Acceptance in a Patron; now in noyse
Of the litigious Rout, has lost his voice.

3

His Zeale is now noe more; his frequent vowes
Are all forgott; the honour of his browes,
     His Laurel, withered;
     His Quill, perfidious,
Dabbles in common Cisternes; ruined
To his first vertue, calls backe what he sed:

4

And runs a madding, with the vulgar Crew;
Retracting his old Principles for new
     And undetermin'd things.
     Poor man! I sett to veiwe
Thy common frailties in his waverings.
Be calme; for Passion tires, on her owne wings,

5

And falls in Dirt; a Spectacle of Scorne
To other men. Be constant; but not borne
     With a blind violence,
     To stand, noe more then turne,
To the Suggestions of imperfect Sence.
Who builds on Sands, has noe safe residence.

ODE XLVIII

     1

     Soe am I slaved by Time,
     I modulate my Rhime,
To the soft Liricke; though I rather Chuse,
Had I the ancient Libertie, my Muse
     Has seen and knowne,
To breath in bigger notes, and raise a Stile

To the Heroicke Number; but my Quill
Is not my owne.

2

I once had to produce
A wittnes, that my Muse
Was noble in her Choice; and had a wing
Worthy the Subject; but alas, I bring
This, to my Shame:
My Poem's are noe more; noe more to boast;
For in the heape of Ruine, they were lost,
Lost, to my name.

3

Let mee confesse a Truth;
The honour of my Youth
Was in those leaves; and if I had a Pride,
It was in them, more then in All beside;
And I may Say
(Retaining Modestie) they were not, in
The common Ranke; few of this Age have bin
Soe pure as they.

4

I would not be my owne
Herald; but this is knowne
To many of cleare Judgment; who have bene
Passionate in the losse. Pardon, the keene
And tender Zeale,
Of an indulgent Father; if it rise
To Frensie, blame not water in my Eyes.
It suits me well.

5

Abortives doe not lacke
Their Tears; and dismall blacke

Attends the Funerall; and may not I
Obliged, in a Paternall Pietie,
     To my best Child,
Utter a Truth untax'd? Noe matter, tho'
Ignorance flatter Follie; it shall goe
     As it was Stiled.

6

     Sleepe in thy Ashes; live
     Beyond all I could give:
Live in thy Fate; and everie Eye shall pay
Its Tribute to thy urne; and sadlie Say:
     Here is interred
A Fathers Joy; who cannot want a Teare
From anie Eye, who sees this Sepulchre
     Which Ruine reared.

7

     This Storie of thy Fate,
     These Tears, shall vindicate;
And yet I doubt not, but againe to bring
Numbers of weight, and mightie Epick's Sing,
     When Time shall raise
Industrious Quills to Meritt. I, till then
Weave out my Time, with an unsteddye Pen,
     A thousand waies.

8

     My better Hopes, here fixe;
     That I shall intermixe,
One Day, when Peace againe our Feilds shall tread,
Something of worth, for all the world to read.
     How farre! the reach
Of Poesie, enfranchised in her Ayme,
May (justlie warranted by vertue) claime!
     What high things teach!

9

Till when: my nummed Feet
In ragged Sockes, forget
Those statelie measures; and contented, I
Draw Slender Odes, to the varietie
Of Chance, and Time.
With these, I please my selfe; and sing away
My weight of Cares, to linger out the Day
In Liricke Rhime.

ODE XLIX

1

I am not limited to a precise
Number, in what I write;
Nor curbe my owne delight
Of Freedome, to be thought more formall wise.
Nor doe I meerlie Strive
To change; but take the next
Which falls to Sence: the Live
Formes of an honest text,
Seekes little to Illustrate its intent;
And wrests in nothing, from the Argument.

2

Though in these Scattered Fancies, I can boast
Noe proper Treatise; for
I catch, at everie hower,
And onlie glance at things; I am not lost
To Studies of more weight;
But Shadow out, by these,
What I would chuse to write,
Were I secure in Ease;
And often touch the String, I would Applye,
Would Time allow, to its full Harmonye.

3

I cannot Subject my Designe to Rhime;
  That is, I cannot fall
  Meerlie to Rhime; and all
My notions hang, to any certaine Chime;
  But to the nearest Sence
  I take a Number fitt;
   And hardlie, for pretence
   Of finer, loose my witt;
For who that has his Passions subdued?
Can bind his Reason, to that Servitude?

4

Man (Lord of Language, great Distinguisher
Of Forme, to what is fitt)
Looseth, if he submitt
To Custome, his Prerogative; may cleare
  All Scruples, and dispose
  Of them by Edict, to
   What ever heele propose;
   They loose theire title, who
Necessitate a Forme, or dwell in words.
Soe are they vassalls made, who were borne Lords.

5

Some (who pretend to witt) ; (Some, I have knowne)
  Imagine all the height
  Of witt, in the Conceipt
Of formall Trifles; these are often Showne
  To common Eyes; who for
  It pussles them, admire;
   And get a Copie, more
   To sooth, then to Desire
Any thing tasting witt; these frequent are,
In this witt-venting Age, where none want Share.

St. 4 All Scruples,]; All Scruple Ms., Grosart.

6

How some racke all their Faculties? and Squeese
      The Juice, of all their Braine!
      In a fastidious Straine
Of words to pussle Men; and can but please
      Themselves, with a thin Ayre.
      What trifle can wee name,
        Soe barren, or soe bare?
      Be it an Anagram,
To stifle all the Life of common witt,
But busies some Men, to be proud in it?

7

Of these, not three I ever saw, has hit
      Within the roade of Sence;
      Nay give em their pretence,
The Latitude they aske. How below witt
      They Stand, I dare not Say;
      Lest I be challenged;
        Uncapable, that way;
      For I am soe indeed;
And tis a Qualitie I not admitt
Within the Region of a noble witt.

ODE L

1

Oh! Doe not warrant Sin, in your Applause!
    Indeed: I saw your Heart:
And you abhorred the Face ont; her witt was
    Beyond a womans part;
    You hardlie had an Art
To keepe backe blushes: Conscious in her Cause.

2

Fye: doe not Say, you love that Spirrit in
    The Sex! Your heart Saies noe;
You cannot valu't, as a Common Sin;
    It is a monster; though
    You would a Vizard throw
Upon such Gestures, as more Masculine.

3

What Man but hates a woman, bold and proud?
    The vertues, which beseeme
That Sex, and makes the few good, that are good,
    Are Silence, Disesteeme
    Of their owne witt, in them,
And Modestie, where All is understoode.

4

Such Petulancies, as you would Contend
    Are pittiful: more then
Prais-meriting (alas!) and you discend
    Below your Judgement, when
    You did applaud it. Men
Sometimes praise ill, where reproofe will not mend.

*   *   *   *

Oh! Doe not Flatter Her, to her owne Sence;
Custome will make her Errors, Impudence.

ODE LI

1

The Cooped Lion, has broke through his Grate,
    And forages abroad;
Whilst frighted villagers, of Danger prate;
    In their amazement woode.
        Consider what
Annoyance may succeed: Hee thirsts for Blood.

2

Soe doth the Ruffian, (fettered in the Brow
    Of awfull modestie)
Pursue his Lusts, when women but allow
    Familiaritie:
        You hardly know
What Mischeife followes, in his Libertie.

3

Make Short his Fetters, by your powerfull Eye;
    And keepe him yet, a Slave,
Chained by (your Beauties Honour) modestie;
    Your Tirrannie, is Brave.
        Ladies: I doe not see
How he can injure you, without your Leave;

4

For Modestie, keeps still inviolate
    The Honour of a name.
And who dare presse, upon that prettye State,
    Which Innocence doth frame?
        Noe Tongue dares prate
To wrong your Honour, or traduce your Fame.

5

Forgett the Fashion of the Times; and Chuse
    Waies, proper to your Sex.

Avoid those franticke Habits, which abuse
　　Your Creditts, and perplex
　　　　You, in the use;
For Fame, will strangelie Glosse upon the Text.

　　　*　*　*　*　*　*

And tis too much Presumption of your Shame
That you are falne, to be Judged in Fame.

ODE LII

　　　1

　　Ill suits that froward Scorne
　　Your Sexe; I am not tyed
　　To woman, in a Forme,
　　Or a Face mortifyed;
　　　　Though I confesse
Some things are ornament; Some nothing lesse.

　　　2

　　Your Silence, doe not Change
　　By vowel, to the worse.
　　Be free; butt doe not range
　　In the frequented Course
　　　　Of Appetite,
And rather trust your vertue, then your Witt.

　　　3

　　Something within you, knowes
　　How to informe you best;
　　Conforme your outward browes,
　　Unto your inward Brest;
　　　　And then appeare,
To informe Men, beyond all Character.

ODE LIII

1

Be not Deceived: I know it by my owne.
  Great Bodies are great Burdens; and incline
  More to the Earth; participating in
A larger Measure, what proportion
   Soever please your Sence;
    Bignes extenuates
  Its proper Faculties, with weights;
And Smaller Bodies, have more Excellence.

2

Like to the Servile Drudge, some noble man
  Has placed, in a great Castle; and you come
  To see the Building; and find everie Roome
Useles to Him; an End is All he can
   Manage; or some remote
    Parlour, his Familye
  May comprehend; whilest others lye
Unswept, till the States come, and wast and rott.

3

Soe am I, in my Selfe; whilst I admire
  Lesse Bodies; where a man is sett soe near
  In all his Parts, contracted as it were
To a Conveniencie; and the Entire
   House, he keeps warme, and Full,
    With his owne proper Store.
  Each office, Hee with Ease, lookes ore;
And lives to use it All; in noe Roome Dull.

4

Reallie, (it may be my owne Disgrace
  But) I am Confident, wee bigger Men
  Have Faculties less knitt, lesse able, then

Weaker Appearances. I doe not praise
    Meer Littlenes; nor from
    All Larger, derogate;
    But by my owne I see, and say't.
I could Lye warmer, in a lesser Roome.

ODE LIV

1

Soe flitts the trembling Needle, round about
    The Compasse; till it fall
Into its loved North; soe clings unto't
    And will not move at all;
Then with a Mutuall Force, these Lovers meet
    In a Magneticke Chaine.
Strange Simpathie! and though wee doe not see't,
    Tis in our Selves as plaine;
      Nor let us wonder why
    The Attractive Power, should fixe
The Iron to its point; soe may wee vexe
    Our Selves perpetuallye.
Rather see everie Creature, pointing forth
Its proper object, as this meets the North.

2

Tis seene by everie Eye, in Common things;
    How apt and Eagerlie
They joyne themselves. Everie occasion brings
    Proofe, to this Propertie.
Tis not alone the Adamant, can boast
    This strange Affinitie;
Not Flowers, nor Trees, nor Birds, nor Beasts are lost,
    But Each, respectivelie,
      Have hidden Flames: and move
    By a strange innate Cause,

To its cheife End; insensible, what drawes
　　　Soe neare a tye of Love,
But loose all Choice; and their Cheife Sence devour
In the strange force of this magneticke Power.

3

These secret workings, in all Bodies are;
　　　And All, at once, are mett
In man; whose motion, more irregular
　　　To all the points, doth flitt;
Yet as Affections objects still propose,
　　　Hee bends, unto the Point:
And though he varie much, and oft, in those;
　　　Some Qualitie of Constraint
　　　　　Urges him to incline,
　　　Hee knowes not how, nor why.
But Hee must bend, to that darke Simpathie,
　　　Which yet unseen, doth shine
Upon his Heart; and passionat'lie move
Him to behold, or Seeke, desire, or Love.

ODE LV

1

Slip on, Sad Infants, of a groneing Time,
　　　Till all your Sand be Spent;
　　　　　Poor Minutes flye;
　　　And yet be innocent;
Or man will Apprehend you, to his Crime,
　　　And filthilye
Abuse you, to the lust of his intent.

2

Or might your carefull Mother, rather joy
　　　In an Abortive brood;

Then have you live
Guiltye of Tears and Blood
In your first Light; and live, but to destroy
What you should give
Order, in all the Creature, as it Stood.

3

Rather pull in your fearfull Heads; and shrinke
Nameles, backe to her wombe,
Then breath this Light.
Let Chaos be a Tombe
To close you, yet unknowne; let Motion winke;
And all the bright
Glories of Day run backe, from whence they come.

4

Ah man, unhappie man! the Infant Day
Peepes, with a blubbered Eye,
To looke upon
The Nights dire Tragedie,
Sad for our Sins; the night in Darke dismay
Puts mourning on
For our Day Crimes, more Sensible then wee.

5

How many Tears for us fall everie night?
Besides those of the Day?
If Pittye faile,
Terror might us Affray,
Correcting winds, and Thunders horrid Light;
But these availe
Not man to Stop one foot, in his owne way.

ODE LVI

1

Tis not to make a Partie; or to joyne
With any Side, that I am what I am.
  All Faction, I abhorre, all Sects disclaime;
And meerly Love of Truth, unto the Shyne
      Of Reason, which I have,
  Guides me; for had I sought, to other Ends,
  I could have bene as popular, as brave
      And had as many freinds,
To support all I undertooke, as they
Who move beyond me now, and more display.

2

For Hee, who setts a valew on his Heart,
  May what he lists Atcheive. I am as free
To either Side, or Anie; as I see
  Truth, to the Skale incline. I have noe part
      Beyond the naturall
  Free use of Reason; and I cannot bend
  To any blast of Time; nor Stoop, nor fall
      To a sinister End;
But must encounter, where my Reason guides,
The Puissance of Any, Either Side.

3

And I am fixt; but yet not rooted in
Opinion, to the hazard of a haire.
  I am not limited to anie Square;
  But free to any better; I have bin
      Perhaps not ever thus;
  And am as Apt, if a Cleare Motive draw
  My Reason, yet to Change. Ime free to chuse,
      And doe not care a Straw,

How others Censure; for I must incline
To truth, as my Faith guides, in her best Shine.

    4
And as I stand, all Reason I yet know
    Warrants the Path I tread in: all I heare
    In controverted Causes, makes it cleare;
For tis not Force of Argument can bow
            Mee, to another forme;
    But a cleare Evidence of Truth; which must
    Shoot liveing raies, to quicken and informe
            The Soule; and wee may trust
Her secret workings. If wee loose this mind,
She doth not faile to worke; but wee are blind.

    5
    How cleare I stand to Truth! and doe not breath
    To any purpose, if I let her goe;
Had I ben mercenarie, there was no
Second respect, but stood to tempt my faith.
            I might have sitt upon
    The wheele of Action, high and Eminent.
    I am not meerlie Dull; I could have done
            By a safe President,
As well as other men; and had I made
But that my End, it had bene noe ill trade.

    6
Had Politicke respects invited mee,
    You cannot thinke, I would have gon this way.
    I am derided; and you will not say,
    I can grow wealthy; Scorne and Povertie
            Attends each Step I tread;
Yet am I fixt. I doe not value Life
Nor name, nor Fortune; neither am I led

By a Demonstrative
Rule, in the Case; nor willinglie admitt
Humane Devices, Subtletye of witt.

7
Though further be it from me, to Affect
That obstinacie, which I must confesse
Is not in nature void; that frowardnes
 Many assume, meerlye to contradict
  I am not in the List,
 Truth be my wittnes; but I looke on things
 With a cleare Eye, a Judgment not possest;
  For prejudice still brings
A moat for Either; but I doe my part
To all I am, with a Clear, Single Heart.

8
If Single Love of Truth; if Innocence;
If to neglect opinion; not to Strive
For popular Applause; if to beleive
From principles, which in themselves convince,
 Be to be factious; if
To labour for an inward Peace, and Sitt
A sad Spectator, of the common greife;
 If to renounce my witt,
 And looke on Quiet meerlie, be a Crime!
I am not wise Enough to observe the Time.

ODE LVII

1

Tis noe new thing, but a worne Maxime, in
    The Schoole of Politickes:
A Subtle opposition; wee have seene
    Many of these state trickes.
        Oh; tis the way to rise!
And wee contemne all morall obstacles:
Give me but Power, I looke at nothing else.
        I'me just, and wise;
Lett the dull honest Christian labour in
His Tracke of vertue. Tis a noble Sin.

2

Stay; whither am I gone? the Times abuse
    Wee never made our Theame;
The misteries in State concerne not us.
    Alas! I did but dreame.
        Mee, Innocence and Truth
Guide, in cleare Paths, without all prejudice
Or rancour. Fancie erring! how it flyes?
        And takes a growth,
To a strange height. I should have ravill'd out
A loome of this, had I not lookt into't.

3

Alas! our Sober numbers never knew
    To taxe men in their Crimes:
Our muse (unapt to Censure) ever flew
    A pitch, below the Times.
        Wee are uncapable,
To sound a Misterie; or dive into
The ocean for a Pearle; a Peeble too
        Suits us as well;
These yeild the common feilds; these wee may gather
Without offence; and these would I chuse rather.

4

Let me be free, though in a meane Estate;
    And live, to use my owne,
Unenvied in my Fortune; rather waite
    Then meet a Joy too soone;
      Direct, and true in all
My purposes; Safe in the brazen tower
Of my owne brest; let Fortune laugh or loure,
      I cannot fall;
Jealous of my owne Passions; free to Truth
And Swayed by nothing or to sleight, or Sooth;

5

But pleased in my retire, my Selfe survay;
    And Studie my owne Heart:
Turne over a new leafe, for everie Day:
    And many things impart,
      Which Common Sence and Eyes
Oft see not. Tis a Speculation
More pleasant, then all else I yet have knowne;
      And Hee that tryes,
With a Discerning Light, shall weare the Spoyles
Of a Selfe-Conquest, fitt to crowne his Toyles.

6

Then kicke the world, and all Selfe Interest;
    Reject all Hopes, and Fears;
Abandon humane witt; and doe not rest
    In the thin Characters
      Of weake, and emptie words;
Bear up; and resigne all, to reassume
A greater Libertie. Oh! let me come.
      My will accords
To gaine that freedome; I will loose Each part
Of man, to see my Selfe, in my owne Heart.

ODE LVIII

Poore man! I am as Dull, as dull can bee;
    Dull in my Selfe, with Sin,
For Sin is heavie; I am darke within;
    And cannot see
My selfe. Poor man! a Cloud, has spred upon
My Soule, and I am lost; I am undone:
    Huge vapour flyes
Betwixt me and my selfe; all Light is gon;
    I am a Chaos growne;
Rise, Sun of Glorie, yet at length arise!

       *   *

Dispell these mists; that I at once may See
My selfe, in my owne Heart; and All, in Thee.

ODE LIX

1

Not, though wee keepe a Soft
Low number; scorne to read our verse;
    Strong Pineons flye aloft,
And haughtie Quills, high Things reherse.
    Mee, better suits to Creepe,
    Then with Icarian winge,
Contrive a scorned Ruine. To the Cheape
Ayre of opinion, will I never Sing;
    I cannot weepe,
Nor Laugh, to Please; I can doe noe such Thinge.

2

Shall I soe farre Submitt
My Reason? perhaps to one lesse?
    Or prostitute my witt,

To a more Customarie Dresse?
I am not borne a Slave.
If Fortune worse contrive,
Nature intended better; yet I have
Somewhat She cannot take, She did not give:
There am I brave;
A Monarch free, though I in fetters Live.

3
Ah, but I must resigne;
For I am not my owne, to Say
Or Doe; nothing of mine
But I submitt, to the worne way
Of Custome. I will write
Full Panegerickes to
Celebrate Justice in our Age: make white
Foule Crimes; and tell Posteritie wee owe
To those, that fight
Soe good a Cause, all wee can Say, or Doe.

4
Yes; I will say it: and
Put of my Nature, for a while:
My witt, to anie hand
Entrust; and sing for a State Smile,
Or potent Countenance.
Tis wisedome, to forgett
Sometimes our Interests; wise men make Chance
A Deitie. Tis madnes to love witt,
May disadvance
A further reach: I'me taught, and I submitt.

5
Were I an Atome, in
The Ages Glasse, I must run free,
Or stop the passage. Men
Are Sands, and run Successivelie;

Each in his way, and Place.
　　　If any make a Stop,
The rest want motion. Each graine, to the Masse
Contributes, to the consummating up
　　　Of the full Glasse;
And as the lowest Slide, soe sinkes the Toppe.

6

　　　But thus I trifle out,
　In weake Surmises, all my Inke;
　　　And loose my better thought,
　Whilest I of Time, or customes thinke.
　　　My numbers, not Enthralled,
　　　I will noe longer Span
By that uncertaine Measure. I have fail'd,
And let some better Liricke, if he can,
　　　Prove it Entailed,
From Theban Lire, and Sweet Dircean Swan.

Goe from me now for many Daies; perchance
Ere I expect, my Quill and I may meet,
On safer Termes, with Honour to advance
Raptures of wonder, to the Royall Seat;
Goe from me far, till then: which if my Song
Erre not with Time, shall not be absent Long.
Deare Muses, wee must part; yet let me give
A verse to Time, in charge of my Desire;
Noe hand, if I am Dead, and these shall live,
Injure a Line, or word, I you require.　　　　　　10
Enjoy with Freedome, all your owne conceit,
Let mine not be infring'd, but Equall Great:
　　For Poets sometimes Fancies bring,

When Readers nothing can discerne;
   And they perhaps, may find something
Shall sett him, in his owne to learne;
   And happilie, a hidden Flame
   Of Honour rests, which never came
Within the Reach of Either; yet more true
Then both, to Judgement. Neither I, nor You   20
   Must Judge our owne.

                        Adieu.

THE ENDE

A POSTSCRIPT

These Poem's are the onlie remaining Testimonie of some howers, which the Author gave up to the Muses; many others from the same Pen, of more consideration, are lost. Hee invites noe man, to the expence of his monie, or Time, upon these Fragments; which were intended, not to the publike Eye, but his owne retired Fancies, to make Light that burthen which some grone under; and had not the request of an endeared Freind prevailed, they had not Exceeded his intention; Nor the world (perhaps) in anie Sence, pittyed Him.

JULY: 17: 1 6 4 7

THE AUTHOR

Scriptorum chorus omnis, amat nemus, et fugit urbe's

THUS, CALMLY did the Antique Poets frame
Felicitie: and gloried in the name
Of Grove-frequenters; thus, old Orpheus sate
By fatall Hebrus: when his suddaine fate
(Convai'd by franticke women) did Surprize
Him, in the flight of Sacred Extasies.
How much unsafe is Solitude? what Joye
Has Groves, or Cities? but Each Equallye
Capable, in Idea. Not the Lire
Which Phebus strung (Phebus was Orpheus Sire)   10
And gave it him; nor his owne verse, nor voice,
Sweet as his Mother's (for noe other Choice
Might ever equall't) could at all deterre
These possess Beldam's, from the Massacre.
That voice, which taught dispersed Trees to move
Into an orderlie, and well pitch'd Grove,
Stopt headie Currents, and made them run sweet;
Gave centred Rocks a Life, & mountains, feet;
Not voice, nor Harpe, which brought againe to Life
From Hell, Euridice, his ravisht wife;   20
And did soe Charme Hells-treeple-headed Hound,
Hee could not use one tongue, or tooth, to wound,
Or wonder at our Poet. What nor Hell
Nor Furies durst Attempt, (I Shame to tell)
Women must Act; but women none durst doe
A crime soe impious, soe unequall too;
But Lust & wine, in women can produce
Such monsters onlie; be it their excuse.
The water (yet proud) Sings; (if Fame not Lye)
And runs, to him a Constant Elegie: 30
Such was the fate of Orpheus.—Calme my verse,
And softer Numbers Spin; whilst I reherse
Titirus, sitting under Beechie Shade;
Pleasing his fancie, in the Joy he made;

For soe he made it his; as what might want
There to delight, or please, his verse did plant.
Here, oft (more pleas'd, then on Augustus Shine)
Hee did enjoy himselfe; and here untwine
The Clewe he twisted there; thus Hee, in groves.
Next, see in-imitable Colin moves   40
Our Admiration. Hee, poore Swaine, in bare
And thin Set Shades did Sing; whil'st (ah) noe care
Was had of all his Numbers; numbers which,
Had they bene sung of old, who knowes how rich
A Fame, had Crown'd him? Had he lived, when
Phillips Great Son (that prodigie of men)
Spread, like Aurora, in the Easterne light,
Hee had not wish'd a Homer for to write
His Storie, but ev'n Peleus Son had sate
A Step below in Fame, as well as Fate.   50
But Hee! poor man, in an ungratefull Age
Neglected lived; still borne downe by the Rage
Of Ignorance; for tis an Easier Thing
To make Trees Leape, and Stones selfe-burthens bring
(As once Amphion to the walls of Thœbes)
Then Stop the giddie Clamouring of Pleb's.
Hee poorlie Dyed; (but vertue cannot Dye)
And scarce had got a Bed, in Death to lye:
Had not a noble Heroe made a Roome,
Heed bene an Epitaph, without a Tombe;   60
For that Hee could not want; whilst verse or witt
Could move a wing, they'd bene obliged to it;
Or Say, the bankrupt Age could none Afford.
Hee left a Stocke, sufficient, on Record.

   Let me then, under my owne Shades content,
Admire their Flights. Hee who lives Innocent
Is wise Enough: where Innocence and witt
Combine, what wonders in that brest are mett?
The Trumpets Clangor, nor the ratling drum,
Noises of warre; nor the more troublesome   70
Rage of the Souldier; nor the golden Spundge

Where Harpies licke the Juice; nor all the plundge
Of Apprehension, shakes, or enters on
The temper of that true Complexion.
Vertue is ever Safe; and wee may See
Loyaltie prized, and depress'd majestie
Enthroned, as glorious as wee whilome have.
These wee may see; if not, the well-met grave
Will shew us more. Hee, who considers that
A Losse, is ignorant to value Fate.   80

   Bring out the Engine quicklie, to undoe
The Partie: triumph in the overthrow
Of Truth and Justice. You the seamles Coat
Have torne; and dipt the Fleece without a Spott
In Cisternes of Profanesse. Ring the Bells!
Y' have done, y' have done the worke. Hee happie dwells
Who more remote, may looke upon the Age
As his owne Mirror; and applye the Rage
Of Tumults to his Passions; Rebells all
To Monarch Reason. These things when I call   90
Unto my private, then I easilie See
Monarchs are Men. Each man's one Monarchie.

   Phlegme, my Complexion, here has plunged me in
A Quick-sand, to disorder the Designe
Of my first Thoughts; and all that I have said
Is but a Ramble, from a Running head,
Perhaps a Rheugme: for tis unnaturall
In the most Sanguine, nere to run at All.
Who knowes Witt, knowes somewhat of madnes Still
(Distempers not, but) tempers the best Quill.   100
Man in his little world, is more by much
Then the great world; who knowes Him, knowes him Such
A Composition of the same mixt Stuffe,
Which who can temper, but is Wise Enough.

1.6.4.7.

95 all that]; all what Ms., Grosart.

POLYLOGIA;
OR, SEVERAL ECLOGES

AN ECLOGE:
SPOKEN BY DAMON, AND AMINTAS!

Non canimus Surdis respondent omnia Silvæ

DAMON: Amintas! (who our northerne feilds makest proud;
             Whose Eye; then Phoebus, more prevents that cloud,
             Now from the Southeast threatning) ah, how long?
             How many Summers since thy glorious Songe
             Our Ayre enricht? growne foggie, since the time
             Strephon contending in an humble Rhime
             His Silva prais'd, to thy Urbanaes Eyes.
             Deare Shepheard, now (if our Societies
             Seeme not unworthy thee) that pipe assaye,
             Which has made Short, even the Longest Daye.   10

AMINTAS: Damon, that Pipe is broke; and Numbers now
             Amintas can noe more; my Braine and Brow
             Is but one Cloud; if Damon, I may heare
             Thy better Notes, I lend a willing Eare.

DAMON: My deare Amintas, Say: what may it be?
             (If a freind may partake) that troubles thee?
             Are thy flockes faint? or doth Alexis faile
             In freindships to thee? or (more Sad then All)
             Is thy Urbana false? a feare, I durst
             Scarce feare! but Love is Apt to feare the worst.   20
             Say Shepheard, to thy freind; what Torture may
             Soe scorch thy Soule, to wash thy Eyes away?

AMINTAS: If Damon, my weake Spirrits may not beare
             Soe great a Burthen, doe not blame a Teare:
             Your feare, alas, is but too safe, too Just;
             Urbana is—is false; and strangelie lost

To her first vowes, a prostitute; or more,
To the Grand Paillard, proud to be his whore.
This, but a part; though, ah! too much by this;
The rest, I cannot Speake; for Damon, tis   30
Soe beyond wonder, such a Prodigie,
It starts a Horror, everie Thought in Mee.

DAMON: May it not Adde Affliction! to lay out
All thy mishap? My deare Amintas doe't;
Whilest I with open Ears, thy Sorrowes gather
Into my brest; we better suit together.
Let me (at lest, in this) thy Rivall prove;
Tis fitt hee Share thy greife, whom thou dost Love.

AMINTAS: The Storie's Long and Sad; but may Appeare,
Perhaps, not tedious to a tender Eare.   40
Yow Damon, are concern'd; your Loyaltie
Makes yow a partner, in the miserie;
And the strict tye of freindship, twixt us two
Emboldens me to utter, what I know.
Thus then it is; our folds and flocks, while ere
To Pan made Sacred; and his Steward here
Next under Him wee honour; and noe knee
But unto him did bend, in fealtie;
His Ivorie Hooke; (made glorious by his Hand)
More then a Scepter, shined ore the Lande;   50
And wee inferiour Swains, were taught to bring
Our Tribute Lambes, and our fleece-offering,
To this Great Shepherd; part of the increase
Which Hee preserved soe many yeare in Peace;
This was, but Damon! now, wee may noe more
Performe, or paye the Duties us'd to fore.

DAMON: Is Pietie a Sin? or Loyaltie
Now made a Crime? unriddle it to mee;
For since I can remember, I was taught
To honour the Great Shepheard; and have brought

My frequent Tributes, with a willing Hand.   61
Who now soe bold, dare his just rights withstand?

AMINTAS: Ah Damon, latelie to another Hee
Imparted Somewhat of his Roialtie.
A cozen of the Blood; of Sex, unfitt
For Soveraigntie; yet Hee allow'd her Sitt
Next to his Throne; unheeding what too Late
Hee now repents, her ill-bestowed State;
For when She now, by favour of his Eye,
Seem'd, to the world, a part of majestie;   70
The giddie Heads, who still delight in Change
Fixe upon Her the Light; and put a Strange
Glorie upon Her; yet, it was but Ayre,
And her owne Pride, made her appeare soe faire;
For all the Nobler Shepherds were afraid
Her Rule might ruine what the other made.
Still our Great Shepherd, to himselfe Secure,
Is pleas'd, with new Addresses made unto Her.
From everie corner of this Iland, flye
Papers, to establish her yonge Majestie;   80
Hee, all the while remisse, is well content
To see how she can manage Government;
Lulled by her Sugred Sayings, and the oft
Repeated vowes, which (ah) She never thought.
Hee, from his owne Hand, gives his Ivorie hooke,
Which even His Father and Himselfe had tooke
Of Pan, with Solemne vow; and now begins
Proud Zephirina to augment her Sins;
For what She only wisht, and durst not Act,
Power, gives her Right; and Justifyes the fact.   90
Now, by himselfe forsaken, many Swains
Leave him (alas), whom kind Shee entertains.
Still her power Spreads; the Axe is now put downe
Unto the Roote. The ruine falls, a Crowne;
Now those who were freinds, or in favour high
To the Great Sheapherd, fall; for Royaltie

Admitts noe Rivall; and Supreme Estate
Nothing Approves, but what it did Create.
What need I tell, Philarchus lost his Head;
Or Mirabella, strangelie banished?   100
Or how Penandro, now her Minion growne,
Must not by him be call'd in Question
For highest Crimes? To offer it, were more
Then Regicide it Selfe had bene before;
And even those few, which did attend Him then,
Rebells denounc't; Himselfe the worst of Men;
That now (alas) he's forc'd (Soe powerles left)
In this remoter Countrie, thus to Shift.

DAMON: Oh the Sad Day! Amintas, wee have seene
          The former Glories of a King and Queene;   110
          Then Zephirina hardly had a Name,
          At most, below any pretence of Claime;
          Alas, what Safetie can our feilds Afforde
          To Him, they must acknowledge yet their Lord?
          Hee thinlie fenced, with Loyall Hearts, may Stand:
          But they (alas) want Armes, to the strong Hand
          Of Zephirina now; our Townes, are weake,
          Our Numbers few, and farre away to seeke.
          This Sought in Time, might have some Refuge bene;
          When His owne Troopes, were full amongst us
                seene;   120
          When noe Power visible could animate
          Aspiring Treasons; now it is too late.
          Now Matho, with an Iron yoake has prest
          Our Loyall Shoulders; now, Hee stands possest
          Of that strong Towne, which by a King once rear'd,
          May be anothers Ruine, to be fear'd.
          What can his Hopes Suggest unto Him here?
          Wee All are Cowed, even Stupifyed with feare.

AMINTAS: Soe, is the Nation all: or rather lost,
          In his neglect; they Careles are, almost;   130

And let the Threatning Billow over run
Their fortunes, willing soe to be undone.
A retchlesnes has now Seiz'd everie Mind;
Or a strange Tumor, newer things to find;
For never greater Disproportion dwell'd
Amongst Minds. All are Sunke, or overswell'd.
Hither, our Maister, confident of Some
Yet Loyall Hearts, encourag'd was to come,
Far from the Reach of Zephirinaes power,
Which everie day, encreases more and more;   140
Her late imperious Summons, She hath sent;
And if it fayle, by force She will Attempt
His Sacred Person; tis alreadie done.
Her Complices, in this Sedition,
Bring in their willing Armes; their Purses ope,
T' exasperate her Rage; and urge a Hope
Of her Establishment. Leavies are made,
And Voluntarie Troopes goe to Her Ayde;
That now her forces, in the feild Appeare
A formidable Armie; and Wee heare   150
Cornigerus the Generall of the rout,
Must bring that Project speedilye about.

DAMON: Alas! what Counsels, may our maister have,
To avoyd this Torrent? and his Honour save?
Our Numbers are too weake, our wealth exhaust,
To Cope with such a Numerous, and vast
Army, as they are made to us by fame.
Amintas, Say: what Succours can Hee frame?

AMINTAS: Tis (ah) but Small: yet all Hee can pursue
Necessitated thus. Hee, with the fewe   160
Willing to serve him, Westward now intend;
Where they perswade, Hee will have many a freind;
However, he resolves at once to run
The hazard of his Life, with Losse of Crowne.
There, his Imperiall Standard will he place,

(If yet it be soe powerfull, as it was)
To call in everie Heart, and everie Hand,
T' assist his Right, and her rude force withstand;
This, his last Refuge, a wan hope, to bring
Himselfe, to former Glories of a Kinge.   170

DAMON: I doe not See, what Succours can be brought,
Worthy of his Necessities, or Thought.
For Zephirina, everie Countie awes
With Edicts Strange, and never heard of Lawes;
Her Ministers, throughout the Kingdome spred,
Are Active, to advance her late-rais'd Head.
All mouths are full of Her; and everie Tongue
In her Names Priviledge, can not speake wronge;
When our Great Maister, but a Byword Stands,
And Groomes dare make a Jest of his Commands. 180
But Say, Amintas, for the Evening calls,
How comes thy bright Urbana to be false?

AMINTAS: That, as a part of Sorrow, to the rest
Then may I adde; and poure out all my brest.
When Zephirina, in her obscure Cell
Lived ere while, Urbana loved her well;
And though She cunning kept it from my Eare,
She wish'd her ever, what wee All now see her;
And her Ambitions did foment, to all
Strange undertakings; that I doe not Call   190
Em worse, for worst they are. Noe sooner was
This Zephirina in the Royall place,
But false Urbana, all her vowes made Light;
Her many former vowes, which Shee had plight:
And with new oaths seal'd, for the single Sway
Of this Usurper joynes; and everie day
Adds to her rule. Urbana Sweeps the round
Of all her Streets, for Ruffians to be found;
And all the Dregs of men, by numerous Poll's,
Swarme in to fill up Zephirinaes Rolls: 200

These Polymorphus leads in, to assist
The new-rais'd Tirranie, of What they List;
And thus Urbana, (not to her owne Lust,
But Zephirinaes Baud) has quitt her Trust.
What shall I more? what yow imagine more,
Urbana is of wicked; thus the Sore
Yow now have seen, which wounds Amintas brest.
What else remains, can never be exprest.

DAMON: Though further Wee removed, not lesse concern'd,
As some have taught; a Dictate, never learn'd 210
By loyall minds, who know noe Limit to
Their Zeale, or a proportion to their vow.
My brest is full as thine, with the same fire;
And what I cannot utter, I admire,
With Horror wounded; a darke Extasie
Runs through my Soule, in everie facultie.

AMINTAS: Ah! Damon! though wee bleed, yet thinke, how more
The Arrow wounds our maister; wee are poore;
And though our Indyviduall Selves may seeme
Near, in our Eyes, wee are of noe Esteeme. 220
Poore Shepherds may be ruin'd, everie Day,
Without a Noyse; and noe Man left to Say
Twas pittye; for their narrow motions are
But in the Sphære, of a Particular.
Princes are set, a Step beyond their fates;
They never suffer Single; formed States,
The Structur's of well setled Polities,
And changed Government, their Exequies
Are ever made; and not the meanest Hee
But falls a Part, in ruin'd Monarchye. 230

DAMON: What may wee doe? the Shepheard is not free
To Sing his Thoughts, under the Tirranie
Of this expected Rage; our humble verse
Now carries Danger, to still Jealous Ears;

Wee must retract, what wee have sung before;
And Numbers raise (which Muses all abhorre)
To Celebrate the Glories, of a late
Usurped Power, and most deformed State.
Sing let me never, Phœbus, if I raise
To thriving Treasons any note of Praise.   240

AMINTAS: Noe matter, Swaine; Apolloes Harpe unstrunge,
Was seen the other Day; and careles hung
Upon the Willowes. Pan, his Syrinx, made
A pipe, has throwne away; and left the Trade.
The Muses Silent; everie Swaine, strucke mute,
And Verses now fall, like untimely fruite.
For what is left, to Sing? our Glorie's gon,
Our Loves are Lost, or not worth thinking on.

DAMON: More happines have wee; (though Miserie
Surround us All) yet in our Loves, wee're free;   250
And Shepheards humble Loves, wee not the least
Of happines determine, if not Best.

AMINTAS: Had Such bene mine; Soe had I happie lived;
My flockes still kept their fold; and I had greived
Noe Strumpets loosenes; then my Pipe had Still
Bene pleasant; now, a worne and wearied Quill.
Damon, noe more; for longer Shadowes fall
From Western Hills, and Shepheards homeward call.

THE SONGE:

1

   Unshorne Apollo! throw away
      That wreath, thy Tresses crowning:
   Thy Daphne withers, from a Bay
      To some poore Shrub: not owning
   Her former verdure. Wee now bring
   A Chaplet of our gathering.

2

   The Bramble and the wood-bine (lived
      Not halfe a day) are twisted,
   Some nettles mixt; as who beleived
      Thy Glorie still existed!
   Or to make finer, wee will trim
   With Marigolds thy Anadem;

3

   For Joy is Dead, and Glorie faint;
      Witt, banished our feilds;
   Say! great Protector! if wee may n't
      Give, as the Season yeilds?
   Or wouldst thow still Bay-crowned Sitt?
   Restore us ours; weele give thee it.

THE END

Idyllia:
THE DISTEMPER
A POEM
REVISED, & ENLARGED
BY THE AUTHOR.

IDYL: 4

Nor wonder, if the loud Prærogative
Scatter our Dust, & licke our Sweat, to Live
With the same Innocence, as Fishes Mudde;
Land Cormorants may Challeng them for food;
Who grasse to Lions? or Slaine Bullocks flings
To Camells? the whole world, through severall Things
Eats her selfe up; the Estrich, may digest
A Broken Rocke, & on a Plough Share feast;
Some Eate the fruits, & some the Juice of Earth
Whose quicke returnes bring second Fodders forth,   10
Fatted, to feed themselves. Arabia yeilds
Noe wonder in her Bird, (if true) which builds
Her funerall Pile, her Cradle; the world, weake,
Reveiwes her Selfe, & what the Ancients Speake
From the first Symbole, Traditorie Truth
Is soe indeed. If wee observe the Growth,
And decay of Things, the world is All
One Phœnix; & makes new originall
From her owne Ashes; as she one Day must
Start, from one flame, new & refined Dust,   20
She, now in parcells, Dictates, to her Earth
The Transmigration of an Entire Birth;
Therfore I must Correct myselfe; to know
Man, but a Feather; if he fall or grow,
Tis but observed, till another Coat
Gives a new Wing; & weare the Eye sore out.
Tis but a mewing Time; what matter if
Cold Gorges, crampe the feet? Our Eyeass Life

Complaines unpittied; we're indeed soe Dull
In the Nest Gutt, wee Crye fasting & full.   30
   Though Tyrranny (big Swolne in all formes,
Vulture, or Moll) doe Swoop or hunt out wormes,
Men borne for bondage; 'tis not in our Choice
How wee shall Bleed, if Blood be made the Price.
And 'tis as easie Smart, to give that Breath
In Ayre, as Earth; resolvd a certaine Death,
For Kings act open-fac'd, but what of late
Wee see pursued, under the Masque of State;
Where fatted fellow creepers Dig new Seams
And catch it, warme layd; delvinge the extreams   40
Of the darke Centre, with an Eager Foot;
And wee are strangled, ere our neighbors know't.
This yet, I'de rather Shun, might I but creepe
To breath in Royall Ayre, then Dye soe Deepe.
   But nothing bootes my fancy; when I span
My selfe to Judgment in the Circle Man;
(And overtoild Affections, wounded Send
To Reason, at his need, my nearest freind)
I boldly looke on Either, and refuse
Neither; but comply to the Genius   50
Directs all forme. I can as well keep bare
To a Cotton Bench, as to a velvet Chaire;
'Tis all one to my Ease, to all the Right
I claime in Man; to all the Benefitt
Of Fortune, (if my former Errors, had
Not lodg'd mee (they, malignant say, I) Madd,
For Sideing is a madnes, where the Hand
Acts to a Somewhat, we but understand
In the Relations) if the Essence be
Resolved through, in the necessitie.   60
I know noe Argument in Reason Springs
T'oppose the forme, by Commonwealths, or Kings;
Nor is't a Sickly bending in the Blood,
But a firme Truth, to what I've understood
From the whole question; which ill stated, Swaies

Us to our owne Affections Severall Waies;
But to the Eye of Reason, (if wee must
Live under Power) all Power is equall Just.
   Man is a kind of Sea-weed (if we may
Run to the Simile, the world, a Sea) .   70
Wee lye weake Spriggs which upon water floate,
Osyers in Ayre, but Corrall at the Root,
Empire low firm'd, a Plant congeal'd, a Rocke
Torne up, a Babble, or a whistle Stalke;
The large Amphibion, now resolv'd, is hung.
To make proud females was our wonder long.
   Empire & State, the formes of Government,
The originall of Power, & the Discent
Are now but Easie Problemes; a Discourse
For unconcerned Women; or what's worse,   80
Taught Children quarrell Crown's: & can declaime
Power, with their Spoone-meat, under any Name;
Can tumble Junius Brutus, & conferre
The Phillipicks, with all our moderne Stirre;
And can name Oligarchy, with more Ease
Then a Loome flitter can Church Hierarchies;
Such Definitions, with their Milke; & prove
Authority, to what their Mothers Love;
And see the Reason, ere they well can prate.
Who Rules the House, to Them, governs the State.   90
   For my owne part, I love a Woeman Witt
As a Tam'd Hare, that strikes a Drumming fitt;
Or the Cag'd Squirrell, with a jing of Bells;
Machanicke Entertaine! & the face Sells
Sometimes at better Rate, where they can top
The commers, with the Tangle of the Shop.
But whither Toothed, run I, in mistake?
May the Sex live long flatterd, for his Sake;
Who put the Witt upon 'em for a Boast,
And got his End, Such Labour, never Lost.   100
   Draw out the Scheme; take the Ascendent right,

97   mistake?] Grosart; mistake Ms.

Jupiter; Venus lost, unto our Sight;
And then read on; wee've whirl'd the Pin of State,
Fraile Axis; & see Power, not Constellate;
Cæsar, (noe starre within our Region knowne
Trust in a knott of Tullies Mourning gowne)
Is but a Wild fire, to wast Senate Raggs,
And Silence Cato, whose too bitter braggs
Of Libertie, Chain'd others in the Quest
And lost his owne, by a new Power opprest.   110
   The Slumbers of our Age, (if we could tell
Them out, broad-wakeing) ancient Dreams reveale;
If Life be little more, tis fond expence
To hang up State, fring'd with a Reverence
For better Curtains; & wrought Pillow's bring
Pownc'd Law, stitched Common-Wealth, & purled King.
More trouble to our Rest, lye downe & Sleepe
The Folly out, which others Laugh or Weepe.

Explanatory Notes

An Address

11-12   "The World's a tottring Stage." A commonplace of the time. See *As You Like It*, II, vii, 139ff.

      "And Mankind . . . Individual." Another such commonplace, that man is a microcosm, incorporating in the individual the whole. See, for this particular variation on the theme, Hobbes's *Leviathan*.

      "Antike." Old.

17   "Coloss." Colossus.

23   "Twelve Centuries." In ancient times, a round number.

34   "sleeke it Faire." Rub it slick, make it smooth.

39   "clawes." Soothes, flatters.

55   "Sisyphean Stones." The stone Sisyphus, shrewd King of Corinth, was doomed to roll up a hill in the underworld, only to have it roll back down again.

60-63   "Shittle-cockes . . . Shell." Children's games, including the blowing of soap bubbles.

91   "Flint-wrapt Niobe." Daughter of Tantalus and wife to Amphion, King of Thebes, Niobe was turned to stone by Zeus, which stone on summer days sheds tears. Her pride in her children brought about their destruction.

108   "Syrte's." Syrtis or Syrtes, the two gulfs in the eastern half of the north coast of Africa, both proverbially dangerous.

120   "Fish-scale, Phœbus." Phoebus, an epithet for Apollo meaning *the bright*. A fish scale is shiny, trifling in comparison.

134   "Trunk-hose." Large, padded breeches, out of date.

135ff.   "The Drum" etc. A reference to the Civil Wars.

148   "the last King." James I.

150   "his fam'd Predecessor." Elizabeth. Note following lines for characterizations of Mary and Henry VIII.

171   "The Great Aurelius." Marcus Aurelius' *Meditations* were translated and published in 1634 by Meric Casaubon. It is likely that Daniel knew the work.

179   "Lucian." Or Lucianus, Greek Sophist and satirist who flourished in the time of Aurelius.

180   "a Dizzard." A fool.

181   "Menippus." Cynic philosopher and satirist of Gadara, Coele-Syria, who flourished *ca.* 60 B.C.

191   "Facete." Facetious, witty.

199   "Accost." Greeting, ability easily to meet people.

200   "Foyle." Fencing ability; here, word-fencing.

220   "Axe." The ax carried by the lictors in the bundle of fasces, used for beheading criminals, the symbol of republican government as opposed to the scepter, the symbol of monarchy, among the Romans. It may also refer to Parliament's rule by force.

      "Gowne." Roman toga worn by consuls. It may likewise refer to the somber dress of the Presbyterians. Thus Daniel expresses his respect for the crown as opposed to the Parliament and republican government.

222 "Royall master." Charles I.

249-250 "Hee that knew ... rest." Socrates, who was said to have remarked after investigation that the only knowledge of which he was certain was that he knew nothing for certain. Perhaps also Solomon.

252 "heightned Peggs up-Scrue." Drinking from peg tankards.

259 "the dull Sisters winke." The Fates, insensible, now dulled by drink.

283 *Ut Surgam Cado.* That I may rise, I fall.

A Vindication of Poesie

It seems unnecessary to explain the references in this poem, except those to poets who are lesser known, or who are referred to by epithet.

2 "Amphion, Orpheus, ... move." Amphion, son of Zeus, built the walls of the city of Thebes in Greece by the music he played on the lyre given him by Hermes. Orpheus, mythical Greek poet, given a lyre by Apollo, was able by the music he made with it to move the stones and make the trees follow him.

3 "Men ... Civilitie." See Sir Philip Sidney's *Defence of Poesie* for best expression of this well-accepted belief.

7 "Mæonides." Homer, thought to have been a native of Maeonia.

8 "Macedons Envie." Alexander the Great, who is said to have wished for a Homer to celebrate his deeds.

10 "Ascrean Pipe." Hesiod's poetical power. Ascra was a town on Mount Helicon, where Hesiod (*ca.* 735 B.C.) was supposed to live.

14 "Ennius." Greek by birth, regarded by Romans as the father of Roman poetry (239-169 B.C.).

15 "Mantuan." Virgil (70-19 B.C.), from Mantua his birthplace.

17 "Euxine Pontus." Ovid, because of some offense, was banished by Augustus to Pontus, whence his letters, *Epistolae ex Ponto.*
"Tirants Lust." Apparently the lust of Augustus.

23 *"o cur vidi."* Oh why have I seen? Words adapted from Ovid's *Tristia,* II, 103-104.

26 "Pharsalia's Trumpet." A reference to the Battle of Pharsalia, where Julius Caesar defeated Pompey in 48 B.C.

27 "Cordubaes Glorie." Lucan, born at Cordoba, Spain, 39 A.D., writer of the *Pharsalia,* a heroic poem celebrating the conflict between Caesar and Pompey. He was compelled by Nero to commit suicide.

33 "Danazar." An error for Sannazaro. Jacopo Sannazaro (1458-1530), Italian writer, author of *Arcadia* (prototype of the prose pastoral), and Latin elegies, eclogues, and epigrams.

34 "Swift Arne." The Arno, chief river of Etruria, Italy.
"Thuscan." Tuscan, from the central Italian duchy of Tuscany.

35 "Swan-clad Po." The phrase is adapted from one of Claudian's Epistles to Sernam (no. 12). The Po, chief river of northern Italy.

37-38 "Muse ... Bartas." Popular French Protestant poet, translated by Joshua Sylvester in the early years of the seventeenth century.

39 "Bellay." Joachim du Bellay, French poet, 1522-1560.

47 "Arcadian Singer." Sir Philip Sidney. Here and in the following lines Sidney is meant as Lord of Penshurst, dying in Belgium.

55ff. "Shepherds Boy." Edmund Spenser.

61ff. "Swan of Avon." Samuel Daniel.

74-75 "& though ... greater glory." That is, his ecclesiastical glory as priest and Dean of St. Paul's.

79-84   Note the references to some of Donne's poems and the pun on his name.
102   "Maye." Thomas May (1595-1650), English poet and historian, who translated Lucan (1627), thus gaining favor with Charles I. He later sided with Parliament, and became secretary to the Long Parliament.
103-114   George Sandys (1578-1644), translator and traveler, had translated Ovid's *Metamorphoses* ("Naso") while living in Virginia ("a wild & remote Land") as Treasurer of the Virginia Company at Jamestown, noted as the first literary work of the English settlers in America. He traveled in Palestine ("holy Ground") and paraphrased the Psalms and the book of Job.
115-120   Reference is to Sir Thomas Overbury's poem, *A Wife,* and the exciting events leading to his death in 1613, involving the notorious intrigue of Lady Essex.
127-132   The names here mentioned are both well- and little-known literary figures of the day. To them are added in the margin of the manuscript, perhaps in Daniel's hand, the names of Godolphin, Cartwright, Beaumont, and Montaigne. Most were "Sons of Ben."

To Time and Honour

9   "Third Edwards Son." Edward the Black Prince, who sacked the cities of Normandy and won the battles of Crécy (1346) and Poitiers (1356).
50   "Falkland." Lucius Cary, Viscount Falkland (1610-1643), one of the "Sons" of Ben, who wrote the fine *Eclogue on the Death of Ben Johnson* in which he, as does George Daniel, praises the "ethic" qualities of Jonson's comedies.
"Digbie." Sir Kenelm Digby (1603-1665), scholar, critic, traveler, wrote on such varied subjects as the *Immortality of the Soul, On the Cure of Wounds,* and a criticism of Sir Thomas Browne's *Religio Medici.*
"Beaumond." Either the dramatist Sir Francis Beaumont (1584-1616) or Sir John Beaumont, his elder brother (1582-1627), the writer of *Bosworth Field.*
"Carew." Thomas Carew (1594?-1639), well-known Cavalier poet.
52   "Maye." See notes to "A Vindication of Poesie."
"Allein." Charles Aleyn (died 1640), a poet of some reputation, author of *The Battles of Crécy and Poitiers* (1632), *The History of Henry VII* (1638), and *The History of Euriolus* (1639); translator of Æneas Sylvius.
"Randolph." Thomas Randolph (1605-1635), poet, dramatist, scholar, wit, and friend of Ben Jonson, he wrote six plays, including *The Muses' Looking-glass.*
"Shirley." James Shirley (1596-1666), well-known dramatist, royalist.
"Rutter." Joseph Rutter (fl. 1635), poet belonging to Ben Jonson's last circle of friends, published *The Shepheard's Holy-Day. A Pastoral Tragi-comoedie Acted before their Majesties at White Hall. With an Elegie on the most noble lady Venetia Digby.* He for a time lived with Sir Kenelm Digby.

A Pastoral Ode

13   "Atticke hangings." Athenian hangings made from the wool famous in the region of Attica.
"Corinthian Plate." Corinthian brass, prized more highly than gold and silver in some parts of the Roman Empire. As Grosart indicates,

Daniel here directly imitates Horace (see Book II, Ode XVIII: *Non ebur neque aureum | Mea renidet in domo lacunar,* etc.).

26   "Tirian." Tyrian, of the ancient Phoenician city of Tyre, on what is now the coast of southern Lebanon, known as Es Sur.

31   "Colchian Bird's." The pheasant, named for the river Phasis in Colchis, an ancient country, comprising what is now the western part of the Georgian SSR. (*Cf.* Horace, Epode II, lines 53ff.)

33   "Ionian Partridge." Horace uses the phrase *"attagen Ionicus,"* meaning perhaps *Ionian heath cock.* (See above reference.)

59   "Scylla, or Charibdis." The rock on the Italian coast opposite Charybdis, the whirlpool off the coast of Sicily. Represented by the ancients as two female monsters; coming to mean two dangers, neither of which can be avoided without coming upon the other.

60   "Isthmus." The word in the Greek means *neck.* Daniel may be playing upon words, referring here to his lady's neck.

The Spring

21ff.   "the Cuckooe" etc. *Cf.* Milton's Sonnet I, "To the Nightingale," and the superstitions associated with the cuckoo, the bird of ill omen for lovers.

26ff.   "The poore wren ... " The bird here says her matins, as it were, singing her "Ceremonious Himne." Contrast her joy with the sorrow of "the hapless Philomel," the nightingale.

Woman Charactred

This poem is Daniel's contribution to the "Character" as literary genre.

3   "Turtle." The dove, of course, noted for loyalty to its mate.

4   "affects." Chooses, takes a fancy to.

16   "Juno might imitate." Juno might imitate her gait and thus improve her carriage; a goddess is recognized by her carriage. (Venus, for instance, in the *Aeneid*.)

Silvia revolted

1   "Devia." One of several small trout streams running through the estate of Beswick and the parish of Kilnwick. Daniel often refers to the stream.

6   "Amintas." Grosart (Vol. I, p. xxiv) thinks Amintas is Fairfax, translator of Tasso.

9   "Urbana." The city lady to be contrasted with "Silvia," the country lady.

38   "reaccrue." Gather back together.

Scorne returned

5   "Glasse." Mirror.

14   "huge Numbers." Verses of exaggeration describing the lady.

16   "fond." Foolish.

Supplanted

1-10   Compare the tone of this with that of Drayton's "To His Coy Love," or his sonnet, "Since there's no help, come, . . ."
16   "Curbed Shoulders." Possibly curved, that is, stooped or bowed.
19-20   "transforme / Her faults perfection." Change her faults into perfection.
26   "Nicotiana." His pipe, literally.

To Nicotiana

Note the play on *rapture:* the smoke from his pipe embraces him.
1   "weele." We will.
11   "poudred Tresses." Powdered tresses, that is, the smoke from the pipe.
22   "Hybla." Three towns of Sicily, from one of which came the famed honey of Hybla; we do not know which.
28   "Alimbecke." *Alembic,* an ancient apparatus used for distillation; hence anything used to distill or refine.
30   "loves Alekimie." Compare Donne's poem entitled, "Loves Alchymie."
31   "be-qualm'd." Becalmed.

An Epode

This poem is in part an imitation of Horace's Epode 2, Book I.
5   "Phebus." Apollo, frequently referred to as the god of song (i.e., poetry) and music.
13   "Squared a way." Set up standards for.
21   "Such, . . . betray." Those who, either from what they do not have or from what they have, betray . . .
24   "Stentor-follies." Stentor, the loud-mouthed herald of the Greeks in the Trojan War, whose voice was as loud as that of fifty men.
45   "Composure." Composition of a poem.
46   "Alloy of Blood." Proper mixture of breeding, blending of proper breeding strains.

To the Memorie of . . . Ben: Jonson

7   "Tribe." The "tribe of Ben," young poets who associated with Jonson and wrote in imitation of him. Daniel says he was of the "tribe."
11-12   Compare Jonson's own poem, "To the Memory of My Beloued the Author Mr. William Shakespeare: and what he hath left vs" as preface to the Folio of 1623 of Shakespeare, lines 17-18: ". . . Soule of the Age / The applause! delight! the wonder of the Stage!"
12   "Informer." Instructor, teacher.
26   "Pandects." Complete codes of laws.

The Dedication of a Poem, now lost

The title suggests that Daniel may have been on the expedition, 1639. But lines 5-10 indicate that he was unable to take part in the wars.
6   "Bellona." Roman goddess of war.

This was placed in the End of the Same Poem

10   "Transitorie." Transitory life.

Ænigma

The poem is a riddle, the answer to which lies in the last line. *Cf.*
Ben Jonson's *Time Vindicated* for an attack on Wither, in the character
of Chronomastix.

1   "Crabbed Stumpe." The word is used in two senses: to mean peevish
or sour-tempered stump (reference is to Wither's satires) and also the
stock of a crab, that is, an apple tree.
"Husbands Care." Farmer's care.

3-4   "dresse / And manure it." Trim and cultivate it.

5   "Impe." A graft.

9   "Seir." Sere, dried up, withered, a play on the name of the poet,
Wither.

19-22   "Thrice Seaven Summers... Juice." Wither had perhaps finished his
very popular *Abuses Stript and Whipt* which were written when he
was about 21 years old, published when he was 25, in 1613. The
reference may well be to these satires.

39   "Medler." *Medlar,* a small tree, whose fruit (to which reference is
made here) is very sour, resembling a crab-apple.

41-44   "and now... Aconite." The tree's latest product (Wither's last poetry)
is a deadly poison like aconitum, common monkshood.

Agonie

15   "thrilled." Used in the physical sense of *shaken, made to vibrate,* or
even in the M.E. sense of *pierce;* thus, *pierced to the marrow.*

17   "Alcides." Hercules, grandson of Alcaeus; reference to the labors of
Hercules.

An Essay

2   "Appolloe." Apollo, which Greek god presided over song and music,
as well as prophecy; hence he was prayed to by poets.

4   "Enterd a Poet." Entered upon the career of poet.

18   "to light." The meaning is clear if we spell it "too."

28   "Minervaes." Roman goddess identified with the Greek Athena, the
personification of thinking power, goddess of wisdom, patroness of the
arts.

29   "giddie Rout." Foolish multitude or the ignorant and unstable mob.

38   "Mnemosyne." Memory, daughter of Uranus (Heaven) and mother of
the Muses by Zeus.

42   "Orpheus." Mythical Greek poet, who is supposed to have lived in
Thrace before the time of the Argonauts, presented the lyre by Apollo,
who rescued his wife Eurydice from Hades by means of his music.
"Linus." Son of Apollo by the princess Psamathe, the personification
of a dirge or lamentation.

43   "Mæonides." Homer.

50   "Cæsar-supported Maro." Augustus Caesar himself was Virgil's patron.

52-53 "Ovid...Change of Things." Ovid who wrote the *Metamorphoses*.
59-60 "And shall the seelie Age...Chaucers Snuffe?" Rustic, humble, plain age...blow upon the charred butt of his burnt-out candle so as to rekindle the flame of poetry.
102 "Dan Geoffrie." Geoffrey Chaucer. "Dan" was a term of respect and often endearment.
105 "Tall Men at Meeter." Excellent rhymers.
"one there was..." Ariosto.

Prevention

60 "Tanais, or Volgha." The Russian rivers Don (Duna) and Volga.
63 "Standish." Stand or case for writing materials.

A Strange Maye

3 "Tempe." Beautiful valley in Thessaly, where Apollo purified himself after slaying the Python; where he chased Daphne, whose metamorphosis gave him the bay-leaf crown.
4 "With bright Enamel." *Cf.* Milton's *Lycidas*, line 139: "quaint enamelled eyes."
27 "Chaos teemed." Infinite space out of which, according to the Ancients, all things arose.
29 "Cancer." Zodiacal sign which the sun enters on June 22.

Freedome

13 "Commission, of the Peace." Justice of the Peace.
16 "Poll' gatherer of the Groats." Possibly, collector of tithes.
27 "Stone-bow." Crossbow for throwing stones.
39-41 "close...free thoughts." *Cf.* Richard Lovelace, "To Althea, from prison": "Stone walls do not a prison make."

Proportion

5 "Apelles." Greek painter to Alexander the Great.
"Titian." Italian painter (1477-1576), master of the Venetian school.
7 "Angelo." Michelangelo (1475-1564), Italian sculptor, painter, architect, and poet of the High Renaissance.
9 "Vandike." Sir Anthony Vandyke (1599-1641), Flemish painter, studied under Rubens, had studios in England after 1632, was court painter to Charles I; frequently referred to by Daniel. Note that this poem in its structure, with five divisions of 14 lines each, broken by rhyming lines of two feet, is itself an example of careful proportion.

The Userper

1-4 "I saw...diverslie." *Cf.* Henry Vaughan's "The World": "I saw eternity the other night."

6-12 "Fixt...live." Note the conventional seventeenth-century division of the orders of life: vegetable, sensitive, and rational.
14 "The Square." Rule, principle or standard.

The Magazine

3 "Sweets, the Phœnix drew." The fabulous Egyptian bird, said to live five hundred years, and to kill herself by sitting on a burning pile of aromatic wood.

Love Platonicke

There are eight short poems under this title, each with its own title. The subject of platonic love was a favorite of the time, especially in the court circles. See Davenant's play, *The Platonick Lovers.*
"Non est forma satis," etc. Verses attributed to Petronius and printed among his fragments. (See Grosart, I, 232.)

To Cinthia converted

15 "Joy, to this Societie." He prizes no joy beyond that of the society of the platonic lovers, or none beyond the association with Cinthia as a platonic lover.

Court-Platonicke

This poem reflects the prevalent belief that the Court, pretending to practice platonic love, was using it as a screen for illicit amours.

To the Reader, of Doctor Brown's booke

Sir Thomas Browne's famous *Pseudodoxia Epidemica: or, Enquiries into Very many received Tenents, And commonly presumed Truths* appeared first in 1646.

Upon an excellent Treatise

Sir Thomas Browne's *Religio Medici* was first published in an unauthorized edition in 1642; first authorized, 1643.
21-29 "though in All...This Authour." Daniel disagrees in some parts with Browne, as Browne would expect, both being defenders of intellectual freedom.
59 "Square." Standard or principle.
67-68 "And All...To such a Freind...pay." These lines indicate that Daniel may have known Browne personally.

To my honored Cozen T:Cr:Esqr.

This poem is directed to Thomas Crompton (see line 9), who provided a poem, "To his honoured friend ye authour upon his Poems," prefixed to the Ms., in which Crompton said of his friend's poems: "This which is paradox I boldly give / Thy memory; when thou art dead thou'lt live." Compare Jonson's "Inviting a friend to supper."

1   "Prudee's name." Presumably a member of the Beswick household.
11 "Lockinton." Beswick is 2 miles northwest from Lockington, now a station on the Hull, Bridlington & Scarborough section of the London & Northeastern Railway.

To the Memorie of the Excellent Dramatique English Poets

This was designed as a preliminary poem for the edition of Beaumont and Fletcher's *Works*, 1647.

6   "Globe." A play on the name of the famous theater where the plays of Beaumont and Fletcher were produced. Daniel probably saw plays in the rebuilt Globe.
39 "Socke, or Buskin." Classical footwear for the actors of comedy and tragedy respectively.
41-42 "Or should the Malice...Theaters." Reference to the closing of London theaters in 1642.
43 "Catharr's." Modern catheters, instruments for withdrawing fluids from the body.

An Ode Upon the incomparable Liricke Poesie

Another version of this poem, seemingly earlier than what is here used as copy text, appears on f.274ʳ of the Ms. It bears the simple title "Upon the Excellent Poems of Mr. George Herbert." It abounds in abbreviations, and the punctuation is somewhat different if not better, but only one word is different from the text here printed: *happie* is used rather than *Glorious* in line 13.

5   "long brail'd." A brail is a thong used to fasten and hold close a hawk's wing; hence the poet's brail has been too lengthy and has thus allowed him to fly awkwardly. (See Grosart, IV, 270-71.)
17-18 "The Royall Prophet...path." The reference is to John Donne, whose poem *The Extasie* is referred to. The epithet, Royal Prophet, is especially apt. Grosart's note refers merely to King David as the Royal Prophet. But a second biblical echo may be intended: a reference to John the Baptist.
32 "vaile." To lower, stoop before, or take off, as a cap.
33 "Horace." Grosart prints *Bocace* in his first version, though the Ms. is quite clearly *Horace*.
    "Casimire." Maciej Kazimierz Sarbiewski (1595-1640?), Polish Jesuit and poet whose epigrams and lyrics gained for him the title of the Polish Horace.

Scattered Fancies

This series of 59 odes and a sort of envoy is dated on its separate title page 1645. Its "Postscript," dated July 17, 1647, tells us that these are the "onlie remaining Testimonie of some howers which the Author gave up to the Muses; many others from the same Pen, of more consideration, are lost." It further tells us that these were not intended for publication but for the poet's "owne retired Fancies, to make Light that burthen which some grone under," and that it was only at the request of a friend that the poet has drawn them together and prepared them, apparently for publication. The arrangement gives some evidence of care: the first ode, for instance, addressed to the reader, expresses the hope and belief, in Horatian manner, that these verses may live; the next five likewise deal with the subject of poetry and the poet's fame; odes eleven through sixteen deal with Nature; twenty-six through twenty-eight are concerned with the poet's picture and the image of Man; thirty through thirty-four deal with the composition of poetry; and so on. Obviously Daniel tried to give his "Fancies" some sort of loose grouping, thus reducing appreciably the "Scattered" effect.

Carmen Protrepticon Lectori

The title translated is "Stimulating Song: to the Reader."
5   "Censure." Judgment.

To the Reader

"long winter of generall Calamitie." The Civil Wars and disturbances, not yet over in 1647.

Ode II

St. 3   "Souce." *Souse,* to drench, dip, soak.

Ode III

St. 1   "Happilie." Haply, by chance.
      "farder fett." farther fetched.

Ode V

Compare Horace's Odes generally, but especially Book I, Odes I and XVI.
St. 1   "Swelling boules." Well-filled cups.

Ode VI

St. 2   "in a twine." In a twist, knot, the act of twining.

Ode VII

St. 1   "Hee comes." This figure, central to the poem, called "monster" (St. 3), "Giant" (St. 13), and "Collosus" (St. 15), is identified with Goliath of Gath (I Samuel, 17) (St. 8), with Satan, as the serpent killed by the infant Hercules and by the infant Christ (*cf.* Milton's *Nativity Ode,* st. xxv) (St. 10), and as Antaeus, who fought with Hercules but revived upon touching the earth, his mother (St. 11). It is perhaps a reference to Oliver Cromwell as a sort of reincarnation of the spirit of evil, representing the same forces as those of the figures indicated.
St. 6   "Gire ... Carre." The circle or circuit of the sun.
St. 15 "Collossus." The statue of Apollo at Rhodes, 120 ft. high, made by Chares, *ca.* 280 B.C.

Ode IX

St. 4   "Ere time ... had flung." Chaos was considered by the neoplatonists as the womb of Nature, the repository of passive and inert matter, whence was created the Cosmos after the creation of Time, creation being the giving of form to formless matter.

St. 9   "The witts ... pleasure." The Ancients who wrote of the Elysian fields.

St. 10 "And raise a Character." Write a "Character," a description or detailed account of the qualities of a type, as Theophrastus did.

Ode X

St. 3   "vast mure of Night." Wall of night.

Ode XI

St. 2   "Hermogenes." Perhaps any good singer. Grosart notes Horace's reference to Hermogenes, a singer in *Satires,* I, 3, 129.

St. 6   "Indian Smoke." Daniel adds tobacco smoking to the Horatian pleasures which he celebrates.

"break the Pipes, lye by." Apparently the novice at smoking frequently broke his pipe. Substitute the word *that* or *which* before "lye" to give meaning. Such ellipses are not uncommon.

Ode XII

St. 1   "Swains ... Southerne Glades." The poets of London.

Ode XIII

Note how this ode is linked with the preceding.

St. 1   "Great Rectors will." Great director's, chief's.

St. 2   "Heliotrope ... Sun." From Greek *helios* (sun) and *trepein* (to turn). Note the play on words.

St. 7   "By silken Clue." Originally *clew* (or *clue*) was the ball of silken thread given by Ariadne to Theseus by which he found his way out of the labyrinth.

St. 10 "the Earth, with Jove made warre." The struggle between Zeus (or Jove) and the Titans, represented best by Prometheus in his desire to gain knowledge of nature for men.

"The Olimpicke wall." The wall around Olympus attacked by the Titans in their war against Zeus. (See, as indicated by Grosart, Virgil's *Georgics,* I, lines 278-83.)

St. 12 "fell the Angells." Note the implied parallel which Daniel sees between the fall of the Titans and that of the Angels in the Christian tradition.

Ode XV

St. 5   "the widdow ... Her mites." See Mark 12:41-44.

Ode XVI

St. 1   "Aurora faire." Goddess of the dawn.

"Active Phebus." Apollo in his capacity as god of the sun.

St. 2   "Dayes best Chorister." Apparently the lark.

St. 4   "I slug it." Lie a-bed.

Ode XVII

St. 2   "flitt ... bayte." A hawking term. The hawk is said to *bayte* when she claps her wings or stoops at prey. (Grosart)

       "Jesses." Hawking term meaning short straps tied around the leg of a hawk.

       "mewed." Caged, as a hawk is mewed.

St. 3   "lime my Selfe." Ensnare myself, as if in birdlime, a sticky substance made from the bark of the holly and spread upon tree limbs to catch small birds.

       "muite." Excrement of birds.

       "Clog." Block fastened to hawks' legs to prevent flight.

Ode XVIII

St. 1   "Thus wee deceive..." Note the connection with the preceding ode. This poem was written on December 21 or 22, the winter solstice. (See St. 11.)

St. 16   "Long Barnabie." The feast of St. Barnabas, June 11, unless transferred because of conflict with movable feasts, coming near the summer solstice.

Ode XX

St. 6   "Emmett in a Cloud." An ant in a cloud. *Cf. Hamlet,* III, ii, 390-99, in which Hamlet persuades Polonius that he sees many shapes in a cloud.

Ode XXI

St. 5   "pussle." Puzzle.

       "Leech." Physician.

St. 6   "M' imposthum'd members." My abscessed limbs or bodily organs.

Ode XXIII

St. 2   "violates the Meads ... Pride." Robs, ravishes.

Ode XXV

St. 1   "Pudora." A name Daniel gives his lady, apparently derived from *puditia,* modesty.

St. 3   "I Nicotiana Sung." See "To Nicotiana. A Rapture," in which the poet playfully turns away from his Pudora and solaces himself with his tobacco pipe.

St. 5   "Rectres." Director or chief, from the masculine *rector.*

Ode XXVI

This ode quite obviously refers humorously to the portrait of the poet in full beard which appears in the manuscript.

St. 1   "mossy Chops." Bearded cheeks.

       "Brother." Sir Thomas Daniel.

       "Glass." Mirror.

Ode XXVII

St. 1 "my Picture." The same portrait as referred to in the preceding ode.

St. 4 "Let everie Leafe . . . part." Let the pages of his book give a true picture of the poet.

St. 5 "beard in Cop'ses." Beard grown in small bushy patches. The references here and heretofore are to the self-portrait inserted into the Ms. of the poet in full beard seated in his study.

Ode XXX

St. 2 "Apollo . . . draught." The sun drank from the sea as he rose.

St. 5 "Squallid owle." Foul and mournful.

Ode XXXI

St. 2 "Phebus . . . Luna pale." The sun as opposed to the moon.

Ode XXXII

St. 1 "Democritus . . . Lunatickes with us." The "laughing philosopher," who regarded all men as mad.

St. 2 "Politicke." Politician or politic man.

St. 4 "much seeing Lucian." Greek rhetorician and satirist, whose view of the world is found in his *Dialogues*.

Ode XXXIV

2-3 "My better Poems." A reference to the burning of his earlier verse. Perhaps he is conscious of the similarity between his loss and that of his "father" Ben Jonson.

Ode XXXV

St. 3 "Heavens greatest Brouch." Greatest star which shines like a brooch on the breast of the night.

Ode XXXVII

26 "Nature contracted, in her Store." Man the microcosm. Note the connection with the two preceding odes and the one following.

Ode XXXVIII

St. 2 "crauling Emmetts . . . Time." Men compared to ants.

Ode XXXIX

St. 1 "Shelfe." A ledge of rocks, a reef or shoal.
"putt / A Sure." Put by as a sure and constant rescue.

Ode XL

St. 3 "pangue." Pang.

St. 4 "unknowing Leech." Ignorant physician.
"prevent." Anticipate.

Ode XLII

St. 5   "Draw our Selves." Could man know himself; the *nosce teipsum* theme so common in the sixteenth and seventeenth centuries.

Ode XLIII

St. 4   "imposthumes Mee." Gives me abscesses.

Ode XLIV

6   "Calenture." Fever.

Ode XLV

St. 3   "Beere." Bier.

Ode XLVI

St. 1   "The orbe." Apparently the circle in the Ptolemaic system from which he can view and understand the whole.
      "To give my Smaller Comprehensions plaine." To present plainly what I understand.
St. 3   "Motley." Mixed-colored garment worn by professional fools.

Ode XLVIII

St. 2   "My Poem's . . . lost." Another reference to the burning of his better poems.

Ode LI

St. 1   "woode." Mad, have lost their minds.

Ode LII

St. 1   "Ill suits . . . Sexe." Froward scorn ill suits your sex.
      "To woman . . . mortifyed." To a woman in a mortified form or face.

Ode LIII

St. 1   "by my owne." Evidently Daniel considered himself overweight.
St. 2   "States come." Rulers come.

Ode LIV

Cf. Donne's "A Valediction: forbidding mourning," in which a different sort of compass holds the lovers together.
St. 2   "Adamant." Originally, *loadstone*, the meaning here.

Ode LV

St. 2   "all the Creature." Created things.
St. 3   "Motion winke." Let motion, the measure of time, stop.

Ode LVI

St. 6   "Politicke respects." Political considerations.

Ode LIX

St. 1 "Icarian winge." Daedalus made wings for himself and his son Icarus so as to escape from Crete; but Icarus, flying too near the sun, allowed the wax to melt that held on his wings and was drowned. (See Ovid, *Metamorphoses*, Book VIII.)

St. 6 "Liricke." Lyric poet.
"Theban Lire." It was said that the ancient Greek city of Thebes was built by Amphion: when he played upon his lyre, the stones moved into place.
"Dircean Swan." Perhaps Pindar. Dirce, wife of Lycus, King of Thebes, was killed by the sons of Antiope, Lycus' former wife. (See Horace's *Odes*, Book IV, Ode 2, in which the poet refers to Pindar as the Dircean Swan, "*Dircaeum ... cycnum.*")

The Author

"*Scriptorum ... urbe's.*" Quoted from Horace: *Epistles*, Book II, 2, 77. The meaning is this: The whole chorus of writers loves the grove and flees the city.

1 "Antique Poets." Primarily Horace, though later echoes in the poem are from Virgil and Ovid.

3-4 "Orpheus ... Hebrus." The mythical Greek poet, having lost his wife, disdained the Thracian women, who tore him to pieces and threw his head into the Hebrus, which carried it to Lesbos. (*Cf.* Virgil's *Georgics*, IV; Milton's *Lycidas*, lines 58-63.)

10 "Phebus." Apollo as god of song and music.

12 "Mother's." His mother was Calliope, the muse of epic poetry.

33 "Titirus." Virgil.

37 "Augustus Shine." Augustus was patron to Virgil; hence, the light or glory of the court of Augustus.

40 "Colin." Spenser.

46 "Phillips Great Son." Alexander the Great.

51 "in an ungratefull Age." Popular belief had it that Spenser died neglected and starved.

59 "noble Heroe made a Roome." The Earl of Essex provided Spenser's elaborate funeral.

60 "Epitaph, without a Tombe." *Cf.* Jonson's "a Moniment, without a tombe" in his lines for the First Folio of Shakespeare.

72 "Harpies licke the Juice." These birds with the heads of maidens, long claws, and faces pale with hunger, twice befoul and consume Aeneas' feast in the Strophades. Perhaps this is Daniel's reference. (See the *Aeneid*, Book III, lines 212ff.)

74 "Complexion." Mixture of the humors (fluids) in the human body, thus the temperament of a person.

83 "seamles Coat." The coat Christ wore at the crucifixion, for which the soldiers cast lots. (See John 19:23-24. Cited by Grosart.)

84 "Fleece without a Spott." The Lamb of God (Grosart). Daniel is comparing Charles I to Christ and bitterly condemning the Puritan uprisings.

93 "Phlegme, my Complexion." My phlegmatic temperament.

97 "Rheugme." Rheum, a cold.

Polylogia

An Ecloge

This is the fourth in a series of five eclogues entitled *Polylogia; or, Several Ecloges.* Following the tradition, it is basically an attack on the political situation.

"*Non canimus . . . Silvæ.*" To no deaf ears we sing; the woods echo everything. (See Virgil, *Eclogue* X, 8.)

2   "Whose Eye, then Phoebus . . . prevents . . ." Amintas' eye, even more than the eye of Phoebus (the sun), comes ahead of that cloud.

28   "Grand Paillard." Great rascal; perhaps as Grosart suggests, John Pym, who was accused of being a rake.

46-53   "To Pan made Sacred . . . Great Shepherd." Pan, god of shepherds, is here (as in Milton's *Lycidas* and elsewhere in pastoral poetry) identified with Christ. The Steward, the Great Shepherd, is the King, who holds his power, by means of his coronation, from Christ.

56   "paye the Duties." The various taxes and levies which were imposed by Charles I; for example, "Ship money."

63   "latelie to another." That is, to Parliament. On May 10, 1641, Charles signed a bill providing that Parliament could be dissolved only by its own vote.

85-87   "his Ivorie hooke . . . had tooke / Of Pan." The King had received his power from Christ at the Coronation.

88   "Zephirina." Parliament.

94   "Unto the Roote." A reference to the "Root-and-Branch" movement of the Presbyterian party who desired the abolition of Episcopacy, "root and branch."

99   "Philarchus lost his Head." Strafford was beheaded May 12, 1641.

100   "Mirabella." The queen mother (mother to Henrietta Maria, Charles's queen), who took refuge in England in 1640, only to be sent back to France.

101   "Penandro." Derived from the Greek, *penta* and *anthropos*, five men, by which is meant the famous "five members" of the House of Commons charged by Charles I with treason, January 3, 1642: Holles, Haselrig, Pym, Hampden, and Strode. (With these Lord Kimbolton of the House of Lords was also charged.) Parliament refused to deliver up the men to Charles, even though he came in person to the Commons and demanded them. Thus was the monarch defied and the civil war begun.

123-125   "Matho . . . a King once rear'd." Charles I, having withdrawn his forces to Yorkshire in the spring of 1642, with a troop of horse tried to get admittance to Hull, where there was large store of munitions. He was denied admission by Sir John Hotham, the governor, whom he charged with treason, but Hotham ("Matho") was supported by Parliament. Hull was founded by Edward I.

137   "Hither." Yorkshire, where the King was in 1642.

151   "Cornigerus the Generall." The Earl of Essex, commander of the forces of Parliament.

161   "Westward." Gloucester.

186   "Urbana loved her well." The urban population supported Parliament.

196   "Usurper." Parliament.

201   "Polymorphus." *Many-formed,* apparently a political opportunist who shifted his loyalties frequently, perhaps Lord Mayor Pennington of London.

214   "admire." Customary seventeenth-century meaning: *wonder at.*

241-246   "Noe matter ... fruite." Daniel laments the restrictions placed upon the arts under the Commonwealth.

243   "Syrinx." An Arcadian nymph, pursued by Pan and made into a tuft of reeds, out of which Pan made his pipes.

257-258   "longer Shadowes ... Westerne Hills." *Cf.* Milton's *Lycidas,* 190-91.

The Songe

St. 1   "Unshorne Apollo." *Cf.* Herrick's "Corinna's Going a Maying," lines 1-2: "presents the god unshorne."
"Daphne." Daughter of the river god who, when pursued by Apollo, was changed into a laurel, the favorite tree of Apollo.

Idyllia

There are five connected idyls in this series.

Idyl: 4

6-7   "the whole world ... up." *Cf. Hamlet,* IV, iii, 20-33.

11-12   "Arabia ... Bird." The phoenix.

15   "Traditorie." Traditive, handed down.

27   "mewing Time." Molting time, change of feathers. Hawking term.

28   "Gorges." The hawk's throat.
"Eyeass Life." An *eyeas* is a nestling or unfledged bird.

30   "Nest Gutt." The womb.

32   "Moll." Mole.

45   "bootes my fancy." Remedies, or relieves my fancy.
"span." Stretch, expand, or reach out.

46   "Circle Man." Man the microcosm.

82   "Spoone-meat." Children's food.

83   "tumble Junius Brutus." That is, play at king killing before they can walk. Lucius Junius Brutus roused the Romans to expel the Tarquins, the Roman kings.

84   "Phillipicks." The Phillipics of Demosthenes, orations denouncing Philip of Macedon, as any acrimonious speeches against a king.

86   "Loome flitter." Weaver.

106   "Tullies." Cicero's.

116   "Pownc'd." Sprinkled as with sand for blotting.
"purled." Adorned, edged with trimming.